Patterns for Success
Taking the Mystery Out of Writing Sentences

Book Four

Rosaline L. Fung

San Joaquin Delta College

VisionKeeper Publishing
visionkeeper@full-moon.com

ACKNOWLEDGMENTS

Many people have contributed to the creation and publication of *Patterns for Success*. I acknowledge my indebtedness to

- Mary Ann Cox, Communication Skills Division Chairperson, for her consistent encouragement

- Anna Villegas, Martha Rice, and Jane Burns, my colleagues, for their suggestions and evaluation

- Ray Pike, my friend and co-author on other projects, for editorial assistance and ongoing support.

Patterns for Success: Taking the Mystery Out of Writing Sentences
Book Four

Copyright©1997 by Rosaline L. Fung. No part of this publication may be reproduced, stored in a retrieval system, or transmitted in any form or by any means, electronic, mechanic, photocopying, recording, or otherwise, without prior written permission of the copyright owner.

Printed in the USA.   1   2   3   4   5   6   7   8   9   0

ISBN 1-890756-05-9

Editor: Raymond F. Pike

Copy Editor: Janet Y. Cheung

Assistant Copy Editor: William Hecht

Graphic Design Coordinator: Judy M. Wood

Production Coordinator: James DeBow

Publisher: VisionKeeper Publishing
　　　　　　6333 Pacific Avenue, Ste. 226
　　　　　　Stockton, CA 95207
　　　　　　(209) 474-6527

Cover Designs: Susan E. Lovotti and Charles R. Young

Patterns for Success
Taking the Mystery Out of Writing Sentences

Book Four

Rosaline L. Fung

DEDICATION

Patterns for Success

is dedicated

to the students

who have the ambition and diligence

to perfect their English language skills

and to the instructors

who have the patience and willingness

to help them.

PREFACE

It may seem odd to assert that the basic patterns of English, the sentences, should be so difficult to teach — especially to English speakers — that we have to create a set of four manuals on constructing sentences. But we must realize that our teaching goal here is effective writing — and writing, the most demanding form of language, is founded on sentence mastery. Usage that is clear and fluent in light conversation or simple spoken transactions in home or street dialects is ineffective for complex analytical expressions in the academic, technical, or business world. A typical remedial student is a headline reader, a TV watcher, a phone user — but neither a serious reader nor a frequent writer. The sentence structures needed to produce educated writing or speech are not "normal" or "native" to these students. Also students are often unfamiliar with the conventions of sentence punctuation. In some ways the remedial writer and the ESL writer face the same problems of learning difficult and demanding sentence patterns as well as setting aside the easy structure of light talk. This is the core of our problem. My solution is to promote sentence mastery through the pattern-repetition-integration methods most commonly used in teaching foreign languages. Ample practice using slot positioning is available in all four manuals, and the instructor decides how much is necessary.

A key aspect of my method consists not only of teaching practical English sentence patterns but also of practicing these patterns until they become habitual. Intensive practice is the only way to make this method work. This practical approach of teaching sentence syntax transfers effectively in due course to teaching paragraph and essay patterns. However, it should be noted that these manuals are meant to be used as supplementary materials for students who need help in the practice of sentence writing. They are supplementary to traditional writing and grammar textbooks though sometimes they use patterns and nomenclature not part of a standard survey of grammar or sentence structure. The emphasis is on practical assistance to students who are not yet fluent and confident in the creation of English sentences. Thus, what these materials provide is not a standard comprehensive survey of either grammar or sentence structure, but pattern practice of the declarative sentence that will assist students who are still having trouble with sentence mastery. Other sentence patterns, such as the interrogative and the imperative, can easily be taught later as variations of the basic declarative mode.

This set of four manuals, then, is designed to improve sentence fluency by identifying frequently used sentence patterns and developing students' familiarity with them through extensive practice. Variations to the basic patterns are included based on the addition of phrases and clauses and the use of sentence combining techniques. Overall, the series moves in a pattern of simple to complex in order to tie in with the common levels of basic studies classes and student performance. **Book One** presents the basic patterns, and **Book Four** presents the most complex developments of the patterns in the series. The students' ability to use simple adjectives or adverbs as modifiers is assumed, and these modifiers are included in the examples without discussion. Students benefit most from the sentence practice when instructors integrate the sentence patterns into the paragraph and essay structures being taught in developmental writing and ESL classes. Whenever appropriate, throughout the series, the notes point out the special usefulness of various sentence structures in writing compositions. Further, special attention is paid to the necessary punctuation in the sentence combinations. Each book is self-contained and may be used separately or as part of the series.

I recognize that pattern practice to develop language habits is not new. But I have not seen the method used systematically outside the teaching of foreign languages. Further, composition teachers almost universally complain about the large number of their students — both native-born and ESL — who struggle with sentence structure. To remedy this lack of sentence mastery, sentence pattern practice is an effective and proven method successfully used by many teachers over the years. But teachers have often had to create their own materials.

These books provide a ready-made resource for students lacking sentence mastery at any level from survival English through transfer-level composition.

- ***Patterns for Success, Book One***, introduces basic English sentence patterns and drills students into using them habitually. Once a basic sentence pattern is mastered, the student is taught to expand the basic thought by adding a prepositional phrase. Coordination using ***and*** and ***but*** and subordination using dependent adverb clauses are introduced.

- ***Patterns for Success, Book Two***, reinforces the patterns taught in **Book One** by offering additional practice of sentence mastery exercises. Aside from introducing the ***that*** clause, **Book Two** offers exercises in pattern expansion using prepositional phrases in different positions. **Book Two** also continues the practice of sentence combining. Coordination is reviewed first followed by subordination using dependent adverb clauses. Finally, subordination using dependent adjective clauses is introduced.

- ***Patterns for Success, Book Three***, first reviews the basic patterns and the pattern expansion with phrases taught in **Book One** and **Book Two**. Aside from introducing the infinitive phrase, **Book Three** offers more complicated variations as a means of sentence expansion. Finally, it offers an extensive review of the methods of coordination and subordination.

- ***Patterns for Success, Book Four***, first reviews the sentence patterns taught in ***Book One, Two, and Three.*** Aside from introducing the gerund phrase and the noun clause, ***Book Four*** goes on to teach more complicated variations of the basic sentence patterns. Throughout the series, the presentation of the basic patterns moves from simple to complex, allowing the instructor to select the book that meets the goals of each course or the individual performance level of each student. Finally, it offers an extensive review of the methods of coordination and subordination.

CONTENTS

CONTENTS

CONTENTS

CONTENTS

SENTENCE PATTERN 1

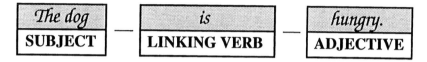

The dog | — | is | — | hungry.
SUBJECT | | LINKING VERB | | ADJECTIVE

This pattern is especially useful when we want to make a value judgment or a general observation. The adjective describes the subject. The linking verb is a connector between the subject and an adjective that shows a characteristic of the subject.

EXAMPLES

SUBJECT	LINKING VERB	ADJECTIVE
The children	are	restless.
The campus	is	beautiful.
Sean's comments	were	encouraging.
Mary's remarks	seem	irrelevant.
The food	is	excellent.

NOTE: Aside from the verb *to be*, there are other verbs that can be used as linking verbs. Following is a list of verbs commonly used as linking verbs.

to appear	to look	to sound
to become	to seem	to stay
to feel	to smell	to taste

© 1997 R. Fung

VARIATION A OF SENTENCE PATTERN 1

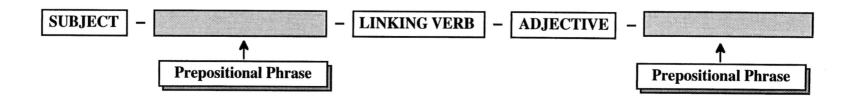

EXAMPLES

SUBJECT	Prepositional Phrase	LINKING VERB	ADJECTIVE	Prepositional Phrase
The children		are	restless	before the show.
The campus	at the corner	is	beautiful.	
Sean's comments	on the report cards	were	encouraging	to his children.
Mary's remarks	at the meeting	seem	irrelevant.	
The food	at the restaurant	is	excellent.	

NOTE: The prepositional phrase after the subject functions as an adjective. The prepositional phrase after the adjective functions as an adverb. These are **OPTIONAL** modifiers that can be added to the sentence whenever appropriate.

The following pages provide practice in writing sentences according to this pattern.

NAME: _____   DATE: _____

	SUBJECT	Prepositional Phrase	LINKING V	ADJECTIVE	Prepositional Phrase
Ex A:	*The students*	*at Delta College*	*became*	*excited*	*about the Christmas Ball.*
Ex B:	*Tom Jones*		*is*	*smart*	*in many ways.*
Ex C:	*Tran Nguyen*	*from Vietnam*	*appears*	*calm*	*in face of danger.*
1.					
2.					
3.					
4.					
5.					
6.					
7.					
8.					
9.					
10.					
11.					
12.					
13.					
14.					

Sentence Pattern 1

NAME: _____

SUBJECT	Prepositional Phrase	LINKING V	ADJECTIVE	Prepositional Phrase
Ex D: *The eggs*	*in the refrigerator*	*smell*	*foul*	*after four weeks.*
15.				
16.				
17.				
18.				
19.				
20.				
21.				
22.				
23.				
24.				
25.				
26.				
27.				
28.				
29.				
30.				

NAME: DATE:

	SUBJECT	Prepositional Phrase	LINKING V	ADJECTIVE	Prepositional Phrase
Ex A:	*The babies*	*at the orphanage*	*appear*	*clean*	*in their old clothes.*
Ex B:	*Most students*	*from China*	*are*	*near-sighted.*	
Ex C:	*The children*	*from Mexico*	*seem*	*happy*	*with the school system.*
1.					
2.					
3.					
4.					
5.					
6.					
7.					
8.					
9.					
10.					
11.					
12.					
13.					
14.					

Sentence Pattern 1

© 1997 R. Fung

NAME: _____

SUBJECT	Prepositional Phrase	LINKING V	ADJECTIVE	Prepositional Phrase
Ex D: *The swimmers*	*from Germany*	*were*	*ready*	*for the Olympics.*
15.				
16.				
17.				
18.				
19.				
20.				
21.				
22.				
23.				
24.				
25.				
26.				
27.				
28.				
29.				
30.				

VARIATION B OF SENTENCE PATTERN 1

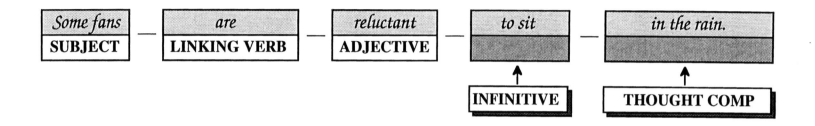

Some fans	*are*	*reluctant*	*to sit*	*in the rain.*
SUBJECT	**LINKING VERB**	**ADJECTIVE**	**INFINITIVE**	**THOUGHT COMP**

This pattern is especially useful when we want to express feelings about an action. The adjective that describes the emotion is followed by an infinitive. An **infinitive** always begins with *to* followed by the basic form of a verb.

NOTE: Here is a list of adjectives describing emotions. Each is followed by an infinitive. These phrases plus the optional thought completer may be used to construct sentences in this pattern.

amazed to see	**happy** to meet	**shocked** to be
anxious to finish	**overjoyed** to see	**sorry** to learn
disappointed to lose	**pleased** to hear	**thrilled** to join
eager to please	**relieved** to know	**unwilling** to give up
glad to see	**reluctant** to leave	**willing** to make

VARIATION B OF SENTENCE PATTERN 1

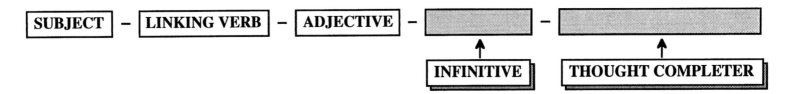

SUBJECT – LINKING VERB – ADJECTIVE – [INFINITIVE] – [THOUGHT COMPLETER]

This pattern is especially useful when we want to express feelings about an action.

EXAMPLES

SUBJECT	LINKING VERB	ADJECTIVE	INFINITIVE	THOUGHT COMPLETER
Some fans	are	willing	to sit	in the rain.
Tom's parents	are	overjoyed	to see	him.
Tanh	is	reluctant	to give up	(the chase).
Mothers	are	willing	to sacrifice	themselves.
The principal	was	relieved	to retire	(after a long career).

NOTE: All the adjectives in the examples express an emotion. Such adjectives are often followed by an infinitive and a thought completer. An infinitive always begins with *to* followed by the basic form of a verb. The thought completer is sometimes **OPTIONAL** as indicated by the phrases in parentheses.

The following pages provide practice in writing sentences according to this pattern.

© 1997 R. Fung

Sentence Pattern 1

NAME: _____   DATE: _____

	SUBJECT	LINKING V	ADJECTIVE	INFINITIVE	THOUGHT COMPLETER
Ex A:	Sonya	is	excited	to meet	her grandmother.
Ex B:	Pedro	was	happy	to be	with his girlfriend.
Ex C:	Lars and Klaus	were	anxious	to go	to the party.
1.					
2.					
3.					
4.					
5.					
6.					
7.					
8.					
9.					
10.					
11.					
12.					
13.					
14.					

NAME: _____

	SUBJECT	LINKING V	ADJECTIVE	INFINITIVE	THOUGHT COMPLETER
Ex D:	*Tuan*	*is*	*relieved*	*to know*	*the test was postponed.*
15.					
16.					
17.					
18.					
19.					
20.					
21.					
22.					
23.					
24.					
25.					
26.					
27.					
28.					
29.					
30.					

NAME: _____   DATE: _____

	SUBJECT	LINKING V	ADJECTIVE	INFINITIVE	THOUGHT COMPLETER
Ex A:	*Loralee*	*was*	*happy*	*to see*	*her husband.*
Ex B:	*The child*	*is*	*determined*	*to keep*	*the toy.*
Ex C:	*The children*	*are*	*eager*	*to win*	*the game.*
1.					
2.					
3.					
4.					
5.					
6.					
7.					
8.					
9.					
10.					
11.					
12.					
13.					
14.					

NAME: _____

	SUBJECT	LINKING V	ADJECTIVE	INFINITIVE	THOUGHT COMPLETER
Ex D:	*Jasmine*	*is*	*excited*	*to get*	*a pet.*
15.					
16.					
17.					
18.					
19.					
20.					
21.					
22.					
23.					
24.					
25.					
26.					
27.					
28.					
29.					
30.					

VARIATION C OF SENTENCE PATTERN 1

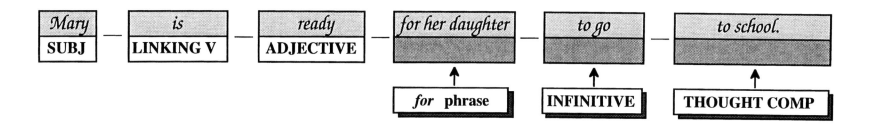

This variation of the basic linking verb pattern allows the reader to express complex thoughts involving emotions. It is accomplished by expanding the adjective structure.

NOTE: In this pattern the adjective that describes an emotion can be followed by a *for* phrase. Here is a list of adjectives describing emotions. Each is followed by an infinitive. The following phrases plus an optional *for* phrase or thought completer may be used to construct sentences in this pattern.

eager . . . to finish	**happy** . . . to do	**disappointed** . . . to see
difficult . . . to study	**pleased** . . . to help	**reluctant** . . . to give
ready . . . to leave	**sorry** . . . to interrupt	**glad** . . . to visit
anxious . . . to drive	**relieved** . . . to take	**sad** . . . to hear
hard . . . to understand	**terrified** . . . to go	**thrilled** . . . to find

VARIATION C OF SENTENCE PATTERN 1

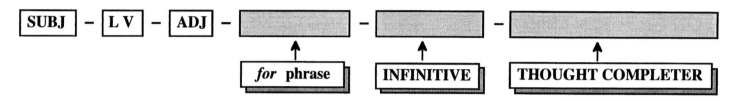

This sentence variation makes the bare-bones sentence much more complex and allows the writer to express complex thoughts.

EXAMPLES

SUBJECT	LINKING V	ADJECTIVE	*for* phrase	INF	THOUGHT COMP
A good man	is	difficult	(for us)	to find	(nowadays).
Tom's parents	are	anxious	for him	to find	a job.
Mary	is	ready	for her daughter	to go	to school.
The students	were	eager	for their teacher	to give	them homework.
The puzzle	was	difficult	(for the boy)	to solve	(under pressure).

> **NOTE:** All the adjectives in the examples express feelings. The expansion in the form of the *for* phrase, the infinitive, and the thought completer gives the sentence meaningful details. Sometimes the *for* phrase or the thought completer is not necessary to complete the meaning of the sentences as indicated by the words in parentheses.

The following pages provide practice in writing sentences according to this pattern.

NAME: _____ DATE: _____

	SUBJECT	L V	ADJECTIVE	*for* PHRASE	INFINITIVE	THOUGHT COMPLETER
Ex A:	*The parents*	*are*	*eager*		*to remodel*	*their house.*
Ex B:	*The mother*	*is*	*pleased*	*for her daughter*	*to finish*	*school.*
Ex C:	*The children*	*are*	*terrified*		*to jump*	*from the diving board.*
1.						
2.						
3.						
4.						
5.						
6.						
7.						
8.						
9.						
10.						
11.						
12.						
13.						
14.						

Sentence Pattern 1

NAME: _____

SUBJECT	L V	ADJECTIVE	*for* PHRASE	INFINITIVE	THOUGHT COMPLETER
Ex D: *John*	*is*	*reluctant*	*for his wife*	*to work*	*at night.*
15.					
16.					
17.					
18.					
19.					
20.					
21.					
22.					
23.					
24.					
25.					
26.					
27.					
28.					
29.					
30.					

NAME: DATE:

	SUBJECT	L V	ADJECTIVE	*for* PHRASE	INFINITIVE	THOUGHT COMPLETER
Ex A:	Tran	is	anxious		to graduate	from college.
Ex B:	Judy	is	happy		to return	to Hawaii.
Ex C:	Minh	is	ready	for her baby	to start	kindergarten.
1.						
2.						
3.						
4.						
5.						
6.						
7.						
8.						
9.						
10.						
11.						
12.						
13.						
14.						

Sentence Pattern 1

NAME: _____

SUBJECT	L V	ADJECTIVE	*for* PHRASE	INFINITIVE	THOUGHT COMPLETER
Ex D: *Peter*	*is*	*pleased*		*to get*	*his new job.*
15.					
16.					
17.					
18.					
19.					
20.					
21.					
22.					
23.					
24.					
25.					
26.					
27.					
28.					
29.					
30.					

VARIATION D OF SENTENCE PATTERN 1

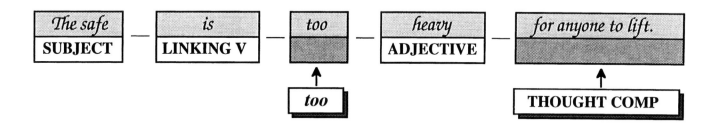

This pattern is especially useful when we want to express an excessive intensity of the adjective that modifies the subject.

NOTE:

- The **subject** is what we are talking about. The subject of the sentence is always a noun or a noun substitute.

- The **linking verb** in this pattern is a connector between the subject and an adjective that shows a characteristic of the subject.

- The **adjective** is the characteristic that describes the noun or noun substitute.

- The **adverb** *too* denotes the excessive intensity of the adjective.

- The **thought completer** explains why *too* is used with the adjective.

VARIATION D OF SENTENCE PATTERN 1

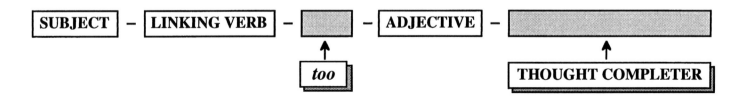

This sentence variation makes the bare-bones sentence much more complex. It allows the writer to expand a simple idea into a complex cause-and-effect relationship.

EXAMPLES

SUBJECT	LINKING V	*too*	ADJECTIVE	THOUGHT COMPLETER
Janet's living room	is	too	small	for a party.
The safe	is	too	heavy	for anyone to lift.
Some job offers	are	too	good	to be true.
The temptation of ice cream	is	too	strong	for most people to resist.
Brian	is	too	young	to drive.

> **NOTE:** The adverb *too* in front of the adjective sets the stage for the thought completer to show the effect of the quality expressed in the adjective.

The following pages provide practice in writing sentences according to this pattern.

© 1997 R. Fung

NAME: _____   DATE: _____

	SUBJECT	LINKING V	*TOO*	ADJECTIVE	THOUGHT COMPLETER
Ex A:	The apartment	is	too	small	for a family of six.
Ex B:	The garlic	is	too	strong	for the child.
Ex C:	The drink	is	too	sweet	to drink.
1.					
2.					
3.					
4.					
5.					
6.					
7.					
8.					
9.					
10.					
11.					
12.					
13.					
14.					

Sentence Pattern 1

NAME:

	SUBJECT	LINKING V	*TOO*	ADJECTIVE	THOUGHT COMPLETER
Ex D:	*The gardener*	*is*	*too*	*lazy*	*for the job.*
15.					
16.					
17.					
18.					
19.					
20.					
21.					
22.					
23.					
24.					
25.					
26.					
27.					
28.					
29.					
30.					

NAME: _____   DATE: _____

	SUBJECT	LINKING V	*TOO*	ADJECTIVE	THOUGHT COMPLETER
Ex A:	The weather	is	too	hot	for anyone to work.
Ex B:	The music	is	too	noisy	to be enjoyable.
Ex C:	The lesson	is	too	difficult	for the students.
1.					
2.					
3.					
4.					
5.					
6.					
7.					
8.					
9.					
10.					
11.					
12.					
13.					
14.					

Sentence Pattern 1

NAME:

SUBJECT	LINKING V	*TOO*	ADJECTIVE	THOUGHT COMPLETER
Ex D: *The play*	*is*	*too*	*tedious*	*to be enjoyed.*
15.				
16.				
17.				
18.				
19.				
20.				
21.				
22.				
23.				
24.				
25.				
26.				
27.				
28.				
29.				
30.				

> ## VARIATION E OF SENTENCE PATTERN 1

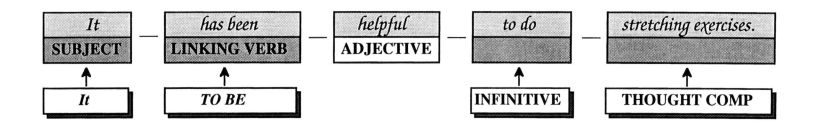

This sentence pattern is especially useful when we want to emphasize our attitudes about an action expressed as an infinitive. The word ***It*** emphasizes our attitude by calling attention to the adjective.

NOTE: Here is a list of adjectives commonly used to describe attitudes. Each adjective is followed by an infinitive. These phrases plus the optional thought completer may be used to construct sentences in this pattern.

careless to drive	**impolite** to interrupt	**sensible** to study
clever to solve	**important** to practice	**silly** to wait
considerate to give	**intelligent** to question	**stupid** to ignore
foolish to scream	**kind** to give	**thoughtful** to help
generous to lend	**rude** to yell	**unreasonable** to insist

VARIATION E OF SENTENCE PATTERN 1

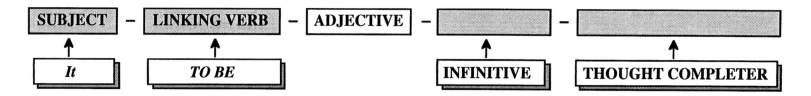

EXAMPLES

It	TO BE	ADJECTIVE	INFINITIVE	THOUGHT COMPLETER
It	has been	helpful	to do	stretching exercises.
It	was	wonderful	to see	Cindy Crawford in person.
It	was	silly	to argue	(over nothing).
It	is	exhilarating	to ride	(on a roller coaster).
It	is	relaxing	to listen	to classical music.

NOTE: Using the word *It* at the beginning of the sentence postpones the specific identification of what we are talking about. This order allows emphasis to fall first on the adjective expressing our attitude. The thought completer is sometimes **OPTIONAL** as indicated by the phrases in parentheses.

The following pages provide practice in writing sentences according to this pattern.

NAME: DATE:

IT	*TO BE*	ADJECTIVE	INFINITIVE	THOUGHT COMPLETER
Ex A: It	was	exciting	to see	my old teacher.
Ex B: It	was	challenging	to return	to school.
Ex C: It	has been	discouraging	to have	a mischievous brother.
1.				
2.				
3.				
4.				
5.				
6.				
7.				
8.				
9.				
10.				
11.				
12.				
13.				
14.				

NAME: _____

IT	TO BE	ADJECTIVE	INFINITIVE	THOUGHT COMPLETER
Ex D: It	was	depressing	to watch	the floods on television.
15.				
16.				
17.				
18.				
19.				
20.				
21.				
22.				
23.				
24.				
25.				
26.				
27.				
28.				
29.				
30.				

NAME: _____   DATE: _____

IT	*TO BE*	ADJECTIVE	INFINITIVE	THOUGHT COMPLETER
Ex A: *It*	*is*	*helpful*	*to have*	*a patient teacher.*
Ex B: *It*	*was*	*demanding*	*to study*	*under strict professors.*
Ex C: *It*	*has been*	*rewarding*	*to teach*	*E.S.L. students.*
1.				
2.				
3.				
4.				
5.				
6.				
7.				
8.				
9.				
10.				
11.				
12.				
13.				
14.				

NAME: _____

IT	*TO BE*	ADJECTIVE	INFINITIVE	THOUGHT COMPLETER
Ex D: *It*	*was*	*unlikely*	*to find*	*Mary in the library.*
15.				
16.				
17.				
18.				
19.				
20.				
21.				
22.				
23.				
24.				
25.				
26.				
27.				
28.				
29.				
30.				

SENTENCE PATTERN 2

The book	*has*	*many chapters.*
SUBJECT	POSSESSION VERB	THOUGHT COMPLETER

This sentence pattern helps us to show ownership or belonging. In composition this sentence pattern allows us to add to the reader's knowledge of the subject by showing what the subject possesses. The thought completer always contains a *noun*.

EXAMPLES

SUBJECT	POSSESSION VERB (*TO HAVE*)	THOUGHT COMPLETER
The play	has	four *acts*.
The application form	has	many *questions*.
The students	have	a great many *books*.
The rainbow	has	seven *colors*.
The old friends	had	a good *visit*.

NOTE: The form of the possession verb changes in tense and number as needed in agreement. Two other common possession verbs are *to possess* and *to own*.

Sentence Pattern 2

VARIATION OF SENTENCE PATTERN 2

SUBJECT – POSSESSION VERB – THOUGHT COMPLETER –

Prepositional Phrase

EXAMPLES

SUBJECT	POSSESSION VERB (TO HAVE)	TOUGHT COMPLETER	Prepositional Phrase
The test	has	a *list*	of vocabulary.
The book	has	a *chapter*	on chemistry.
The application form	has	a *number*	of questions.
The old friends	had	a good *chat*	at the park.
The students	have	many *problems*	with their assignments.

NOTE: The prepositional phrase after the thought completer functions as an adjective. The prepositional phrase is an **OPTIONAL** modifier and may be added to the sentence whenever appropriate.

The following pages provide practice in writing sentences according to this pattern.

NAME: _____   DATE: _____

	SUBJECT	POSSESSION VERB	THOUGHT COMPLETER	Prepositional Phrase
Ex A:	*A centipede*	*has*	*many **legs**.*	
Ex B:	*The old woman*	*had*	*wonderful **memories***	*of her married life.*
Ex C:	*Old people*	*have*	*many **challenges***	*in life.*
1.				
2.				
3.				
4.				
5.				
6.				
7.				
8.				
9.				
10.				
11.				
12.				
13.				
14.				

Sentence Pattern 2

NAME:

	SUBJECT	POSSESSION VERB	THOUGHT COMPLETER	Prepositional Phrase
Ex D:	*The test*	*has*	*several difficult* **questions**	*on Physics.*
15.				
16.				
17.				
18.				
19.				
20.				
21.				
22.				
23.				
24.				
25.				
26.				
27.				
28.				
29.				
30.				

NAME: _____   DATE: _____

	SUBJECT	POSSESSION VERB	THOUGHT COMPLETER	Prepositional Phrase
Ex A:	Tom's parents	have	bad **eyesight**.	
Ex B:	The mother	has	great **plans**	for her baby.
Ex C:	Lola	has	long **hair**.	
1.				
2.				
3.				
4.				
5.				
6.				
7.				
8.				
9.				
10.				
11.				
12.				
13.				
14.				

Sentence Pattern 2

NAME:

SUBJECT	POSSESSION VERB	THOUGHT COMPLETER	Prepositional Phrase
Ex D: *Delta College*	*has*	*an excellent **library***	*on campus.*
15.			
16.			
17.			
18.			
19.			
20.			
21.			
22.			
23.			
24.			
25.			
26.			
27.			
28.			
29.			
30.			

SENTENCE PATTERN 3

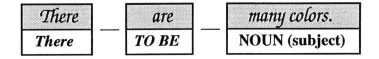

This common pattern is useful when we want to call attention to a subject that is not in its normal sentence position. The word *There* acts as a pointer or an arrow directing attention to the subject at the end of the sentence. Thus, the different forms of *to be* agree in number with the **noun (subject)** at the end of the sentence.

EXAMPLES

There	*TO BE*	NOUN (subject)
There	are	many *stars*.
There	is	a big *problem*.
There	will be	another *conference*.
There	is	a *rainbow*.
There	are	many different *radio stations*.

NOTE: This sentence pattern inverts the usual English sentence order. Instead of beginning with the subject, the sentence begins with the word *There* followed by a form of *to be*. The **noun (subject)** comes at the end of the sentence.

© 1997 R. Fung

Sentence Pattern 3

VARIATION OF SENTENCE PATTERN 3

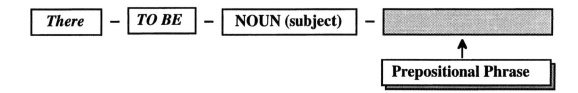

EXAMPLES

There	*TO BE*	NOUN (subject)	Prepositional Phrase
There	are	many *stars*	in the universe.
There	is	a big *problem*	at the office.
There	will be	another *conference*	in the fall.
There	is	a *rainbow*	in the sky.
There	are	many different *radio stations*	in San Francisco.

NOTE: The prepositional phrase after the **noun (subject)** functions as an adjective. It adds to the meaning of what we are talking about.

The following pages provide practice in writing sentences according to this pattern.

NAME: _____   DATE: _____

	THERE	*TO BE*	NOUN (SUBJECT)	Prepositional Phrase
Ex A:	*There*	*are*	*many cars*	*on the freeway.*
Ex B:	*There*	*were*	*many children*	*in the park.*
Ex C:	*There*	*is*	*no solution*	*to this problem.*
1.				
2.				
3.				
4.				
5.				
6.				
7.				
8.				
9.				
10.				
11.				
12.				
13.				
14.				

Sentence Pattern 3

NAME:

THERE	*TO BE*	NOUN (SUBJECT)	Prepositional Phrase
Ex D: *There*	are	many **names**	on the petition list.
15.			
16.			
17.			
18.			
19.			
20.			
21.			
22.			
23.			
24.			
25.			
26.			
27.			
28.			
29.			
30.			

NAME: DATE:

THERE	TO BE	NOUN (SUBJECT)	Prepositional Phrase
Ex A: There	is	a TV	in the classroom.
Ex B: There	are	many computers	in the lab.
Ex C: There	are	many instructors	at Delta College.
1.			
2.			
3.			
4.			
5.			
6.			
7.			
8.			
9.			
10.			
11.			
12.			
13.			
14.			

Sentence Pattern 3

NAME: _____

THERE	TO BE	NOUN (SUBJECT)	Prepositional Phrase
Ex D: *There*	*are*	*many political* **holidays**	*in China.*
15.			
16.			
17.			
18.			
19.			
20.			
21.			
22.			
23.			
24.			
25.			
26.			
27.			
28.			
29.			
30.			

SENTENCE PATTERN 4

Janet Jackson	—	*is*	—	*a singer.*
SUBJECT		**LINKING VERB**		**Predicate NOUN**

This pattern is especially useful when we want to give important additional information about the subject by equating it with something else.

EXAMPLES

SUBJECT	LINKING VERB	Predicate NOUN
These students	are	math *majors*.
The shortest student	is	a soccer *player*.
Baby Jane	is being	a *horror*.
The student actors	are	great *performers*.
The chemistry test	is	a big *challenge*.

NOTE: The linking verb acts as an equal sign connecting the subject to the **predicate noun**. The **predicate noun** adds to the subject by showing a different aspect of it.

Sentence Pattern 4

© 1997 R. Fung

VARIATION A OF SENTENCE PATTERN 4

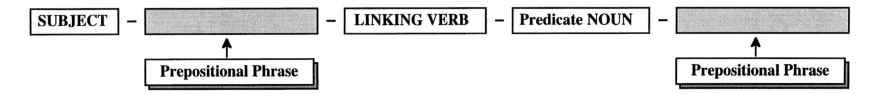

SUBJECT — [Prepositional Phrase] — LINKING VERB — Predicate NOUN — [Prepositional Phrase]

EXAMPLES

SUBJECT	Prepositional Phrase	LINKING VERB	Predicate NOUN	Prepositional Phrase
Tanh		is	an *actor*	at the Civic Theater.
Tom's sister		is	a *pianist*.	
The young lady	in the leotards	was	a *competitor*	at the Olympics.
Jane		is	a *brunette*.	
Sherwood Mall		is	a *shopping center*	in Stockton.

NOTE: The prepositional phrase after the subject and the one after the **predicate noun** both function as adjectives. These are **OPTIONAL** modifiers that can be added to this sentence pattern whenever appropriate.

The following pages provide practice in writing sentences according to this pattern.

NAME: DATE:

	SUBJECT	Prepositional Phrase	LINKING V	PREDICATE NOUN	Prepositional Phrase
Ex A:	*Kirsten*	*from Denmark*	*is*	**a friend**	*of mine.*
Ex B:	*Her sister*		*was*	**a nurse**	*in her own country.*
Ex C:	*America Online*		*is*	*a popular* **service**	*among college students.*
1.					
2.					
3.					
4.					
5.					
6.					
7.					
8.					
9.					
10.					
11.					
12.					
13.					
14.					

Sentence Pattern 4

NAME:

	SUBJECT	Prepositional Phrase	LINKING V	PREDICATE NOUN	Prepositional Phrase
Ex D:	*The baby*	*of Janet and Stewart*	*is*	*a joy*	*to the grandparents.*
15.					
16.					
17.					
18.					
19.					
20.					
21.					
22.					
23.					
24.					
25.					
26.					
27.					
28.					
29.					
30.					

NAME: DATE:

	SUBJECT	Prepositional Phrase	LINKING V	PREDICATE NOUN	Prepositional Phrase
Ex A:	*Vincent Lee*		*is*	*a cancer* **patient**	*at Kaiser Permanente.*
Ex B:	*Louis*		*is*	*a corporate* **lawyer**	*in San Francisco.*
Ex C:	*All the nurses*	*at the free clinic*	*are*	**angels**	*of mercy.*
1.					
2.					
3.					
4.					
5.					
6.					
7.					
8.					
9.					
10.					
11.					
12.					
13.					
14.					

Sentence Pattern 4

NAME: _____

SUBJECT	Prepositional Phrase	LINKING V	PREDICATE NOUN	Prepositional Phrase
Ex D: *John Molini*	*of Linden*	*is*	*a chemistry* **professor**	*at Sacramento State University.*
15.				
16.				
17.				
18.				
19.				
20.				
21.				
22.				
23.				
24.				
25.				
26.				
27.				
28.				
29.				
30.				

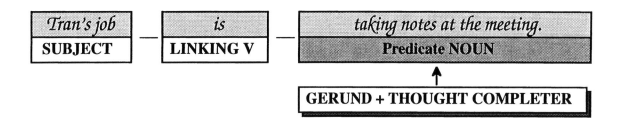

VARIATION B OF SENTENCE PATTERN 4

In composition this sentence pattern helps us to further develop the subject by showing a different aspect of it. A **gerund** plus a **thought completer** substitutes for the **predicate noun**.

NOTE: A **gerund** is the *-ing* form of the verb used as a noun. Following is a list of gerunds that may be used to construct sentences in this pattern.

acting	finding	seeing
being	getting	sleeping
cleaning	hanging	singing
cooking	knowing	taking
driving	listening	walking
eating	making	writing

Sentence Pattern 4

EXAMPLES

SUBJECT	LINKING VERB	GERUND + THOUGHT COMPLETER
Tom's misfortune	is	*contracting* AIDS.
Tran's job	is	*taking* notes at the meeting.
Minh's good point	is	*accepting* the truth about her children.
Joe's tragedy	is	*losing* his leg in the car accident.
Tom's greatest happiness	was	*becoming* an Olympic athlete.

NOTE: In this pattern the **predicate noun** is replaced by a **gerund** plus a **thought completer**.

The following pages provide practice in writing sentences according to this pattern.

NAME: _____   DATE: _____

	SUBJECT	LINKING VERB	GERUND + THOUGHT COMPLETER
Ex A:	*Peter's goal*	*is*	***becoming** a disc jockey.*
Ex B:	*Sandra's success*	*is*	***losing** ten pounds.*
Ex C:	*The manager's job*	*is*	***training** the staff.*
1.			
2.			
3.			
4.			
5.			
6.			
7.			
8.			
9.			
10.			
11.			
12.			
13.			
14.			

Sentence Pattern 4

NAME:

	SUBJECT	LINKING VERB	GERUND + THOUGHT COMPLETER
Ex D:	*Tom's good fortune*	*is*	***winning** the lottery.*
15.			
16.			
17.			
18.			
19.			
20.			
21.			
22.			
23.			
24.			
25.			
26.			
27.			
28.			
29.			
30.			

NAME: _____   DATE: _____

	SUBJECT	LINKING VERB	GERUND + THOUGHT COMPLETER
Ex A:	*Julie's weakness*	*is*	***over-eating*** *all the time.*
Ex B:	*Minh's satisfaction*	*is*	***seeing*** *her children grow.*
Ex C:	*The student's aim*	*is*	***passing*** *the Exit Test.*
1.			
2.			
3.			
4.			
5.			
6.			
7.			
8.			
9.			
10.			
11.			
12.			
13.			
14.			

Sentence Pattern 4

NAME:

SUBJECT	LINKING VERB	GERUND + THOUGHT COMPLETER
Ex D: *Judy's responsibility*	*is*	*typing* the script.
15.		
16.		
17.		
18.		
19.		
20.		
21.		
22.		
23.		
24.		
25.		
26.		
27.		
28.		
29.		
30.		

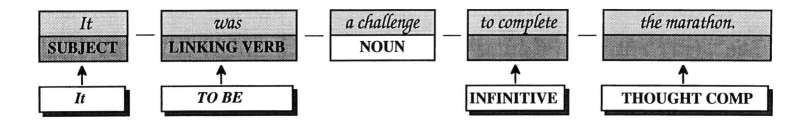

VARIATION C OF SENTENCE PATTERN 4

It	*was*	*a challenge*	*to complete*	*the marathon.*
SUBJECT	LINKING VERB	NOUN		
↑	↑		↑	↑
It	*TO BE*		INFINITIVE	THOUGHT COMP

This sentence pattern is especially useful when we want to make a value judgment about an action expressed as an infinitive.

> **NOTE:** In this pattern the word *It* points to the value judgment expressed by the noun and any of its modifiers. Here is a list of phrases offering value judgments about an infinitive. These phrases plus an optional thought completer may be used to construct sentences in this pattern.
>
> | | | |
> |---|---|---|
> | a **thoughtful act** to help | a **disappointment** to lose | a **stupid move** to run |
> | a **blessing** to have | a **disaster** to cook | a **sensible plan** to save |
> | a **challenge** to win | a **bad idea** to buy | a **pain** to write |
> | a **crime** to murder | a **joy** to see | a **wonderful idea** to travel |
> | a **burden** to have | a **mistake** to cheat | an **unkind statement** to make |

Sentence Pattern 4

VARIATION C OF SENTENCE PATTERN 4

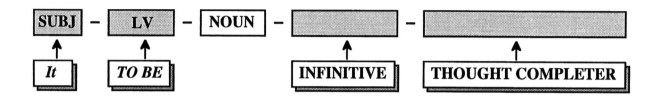

EXAMPLES

IT	TO BE	NOUN	INFINITIVE	THOUGHT COMPLETER
It	is	a blessing	to have	children.
It	is	a sin	to tell	a lie.
It	was	a challenge	to complete	the marathon.
It	is	a burden	to have	a pet.
It	was	a pleasure	to work	with you.

NOTE: Using the word *It* at the beginning of the sentence postpones the specific identification of what we are talking about. This allows emphasis to fall first on our value judgment. The infinitive plus the thought completer identify the action that is evaluated.

The following pages provide practice in writing sentences according to this pattern.

NAME: DATE:

	IT	*TO BE*	NOUN	INFINITIVE	THOUGHT COMPLETER
Ex A:	It	was	a disaster	to drive	in Los Angeles.
Ex B:	It	was	a disappointment	to lose	the game.
Ex C:	It	was	a mistake	to eat	at this restaurant.
1.					
2.					
3.					
4.					
5.					
6.					
7.					
8.					
9.					
10.					
11.					
12.					
13.					
14.					

Sentence Pattern 4

NAME: _____

IT	*TO BE*	NOUN	INFINITIVE	THOUGHT COMPLETER
Ex D: *It*	*was*	*a good idea*	*to postpone*	*the trip.*
15.				
16.				
17.				
18.				
19.				
20.				
21.				
22.				
23.				
24.				
25.				
26.				
27.				
28.				
29.				
30.				

NAME: _____   DATE: _____

	IT	*TO BE*	NOUN	INFINITIVE	THOUGHT COMPLETER
Ex A:	It	was	a sad sight	to see	the forest fire.
Ex B:	It	was	a tragedy	to hit	the little girl.
Ex C:	It	has been	a major victory	to beat	the life-long opponent.
1.					
2.					
3.					
4.					
5.					
6.					
7.					
8.					
9.					
10.					
11.					
12.					
13.					
14.					

Sentence Pattern 4

© 1997 R. Fung

NAME: _____

IT	*TO BE*	NOUN	INFINITIVE	THOUGHT COMPLETER
Ex D: *It*	*was*	*a joy*	*to have*	*good friends.*
15.				
16.				
17.				
18.				
19.				
20.				
21.				
22.				
23.				
24.				
25.				
26.				
27.				
28.				
29.				
30.				

Sentence Pattern 5

SENTENCE PATTERN 5

Damien		*rode*		*his bike.*
SUBJECT	—	VERB (transitive)	—	DIRECT OBJECT

This pattern is especially useful when we want to show the action of the verb moving from the subject to the object.

EXAMPLES

SUBJECT	VERB (transitive)	DIRECT OBJECT
John	left	his wife.
Mary	ate	the cake.
The professor	wrote	a book.

NOTE: In this pattern all the verbs are transitive verbs. This means that each of these verbs takes a direct object. We can locate the direct object by asking ***whom*?** or ***what*?** after the verb as illustrated in the following graphic. The answer to the question is the direct object.

SUBJECT	VERB (transitive)	DIRECT OBJECT
John	left *(whom?)*	his wife.
Mary	ate *(what?)*	the cake.
The professor	wrote *(what?)*	a book.

VARIATION A OF SENTENCE PATTERN 5

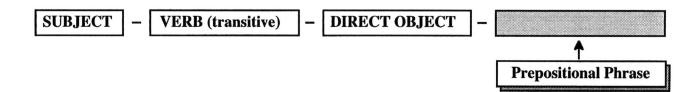

EXAMPLES

SUBJECT	VERB (transitive)	DIRECT OBJECT	Prepositional Phrase
John	left	his wife	in Germany.
Mary	ate	the cake	after dinner.
The professor	wrote	a book	for his class.
Joe	sent	a message	to his friends.
Mark	trapped	a squirrel	in the field.

NOTE: In this pattern the verb is a transitive verb. The action moves from the subject to the direct object. Both the subject and the direct object are necessary to complete the thought of the sentence. The prepositional phrase is an **OPTIONAL** modifier used to expand the meaning of the sentence.

The following pages provide practice in writing sentences according to this pattern.

Sentence Pattern 5

NAME: _____   DATE: _____

	SUBJECT	VERB (TRANSITIVE)	DIRECT OBJECT	Prepositional Phrase
Ex A:	Elizabeth	left	her cousin	in the park.
Ex B:	Joseph	devoured	the whole chicken	after work.
Ex C:	The football players	completed	their exercises	in a hurry.
1.				
2.				
3.				
4.				
5.				
6.				
7.				
8.				
9.				
10.				
11.				
12.				
13.				
14.				

NAME:

	SUBJECT	VERB (TRANSITIVE)	DIRECT OBJECT	Prepositional Phrase
Ex D:	*Kristine*	*typed*	*her story*	*for her creative writing class.*
15.				
16.				
17.				
18.				
19.				
20.				
21.				
22.				
23.				
24.				
25.				
26.				
27.				
28.				
29.				
30.				

NAME: _____   DATE: _____

	SUBJECT	VERB (TRANSITIVE)	DIRECT OBJECT	Prepositional Phrase
Ex A:	Christine	memorized	her lines	for the play.
Ex B:	Minh	forgot	her lines	at the last performance.
Ex C:	Tran	treated	his friends	to dinner.
1.				
2.				
3.				
4.				
5.				
6.				
7.				
8.				
9.				
10.				
11.				
12.				
13.				
14.				

Sentence Pattern 5

© 1997 R. Fung

NAME:

	SUBJECT	VERB (TRANSITIVE)	DIRECT OBJECT	Prepositional Phrase
Ex D:	*Brian*	*learned*	*the alphabet*	*in one day.*
15.				
16.				
17.				
18.				
19.				
20.				
21.				
22.				
23.				
24.				
25.				
26.				
27.				
28.				
29.				
30.				

REVIEW OF VARIATION A OF SENTENCE PATTERN 5

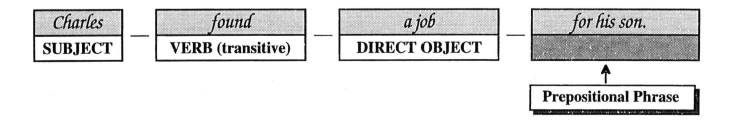

EXAMPLES

SUBJECT	VERB (transitive)	DIRECT OBJECT	Prepositional Phrase
Mrs. Lam	sent	a message	to her husband.
John	told	the bad news	to his sister.
Jane	mailed	a package	to her son.
The Chinese lady	bought	a dress	for her daughter.
The old man	built	a cottage	for the family.

NOTE: The prepositional phrase in these sentences begin with either *to* or *for*. The phrases indicate *to whom* or *for whom* the action of the verb is done. Each of these sentences may be re-written with an indirect object in place of the prepositional phrase as illustrated in the examples on the following page.

VARIATION B OF SENTENCE PATTERN 5

| SUBJECT | – | VERB (transitive) | – | INDIRECT OBJECT | – | DIRECT OBJECT |

The indirect object is a noun or pronoun placed in front of the direct object. It indicates *to whom* or *for whom* the action of the verb is done. The preposition *to* or *for* is implied and understood.

EXAMPLES

SUBJECT	VERB (transitive)	INDIRECT OBJECT	DIRECT OBJECT
Mrs. Lam	sent	her husband	a message.
John	told	his sister	the bad news.
Jane	mailed	her son	a package.
The Chinese lady	bought	her daughter	a dress.
The father	built	the family	a cottage.

NOTE: Here is a list of verbs commonly used in this sentence pattern variation.

build	do	grant	save	teach
buy	find	leave	send	tell
cook	give	owe	show	write

The following pages provide practice in writing sentences according to this pattern.

© 1997 R. Fung

NAME: DATE:

	SUBJECT	VERB (TRANSITIVE)	INDIRECT OBJECT	DIRECT OBJECT
Ex A:	*The teacher*	*read*	*the children*	*a story.*
Ex B:	*Mary*	*told*	*her friend*	*a secret.*
Ex C:	*Tom's ex-wife*	*sent*	*him*	*good wishes.*
1.				
2.				
3.				
4.				
5.				
6.				
7.				
8.				
9.				
10.				
11.				
12.				
13.				
14.				

Sentence Pattern 5

NAME:

	SUBJECT	VERB (TRANSITIVE)	INDIRECT OBJECT	DIRECT OBJECT
Ex D:	*The President*	*granted*	*the murderer*	*a pardon.*
15.				
16.				
17.				
18.				
19.				
20.				
21.				
22.				
23.				
24.				
25.				
26.				
27.				
28.				
29.				
30.				

NAME: _____ DATE: _____

	SUBJECT	VERB (TRANSITIVE)	INDIRECT OBJECT	DIRECT OBJECT
Ex A:	*The father*	*gave*	*the boy*	*a spanking.*
Ex B:	*The lottery*	*gives*	*many people*	*false hope.*
Ex C:	*The lie*	*cost*	*Tom*	*his job.*
1.				
2.				
3.				
4.				
5.				
6.				
7.				
8.				
9.				
10.				
11.				
12.				
13.				
14.				

Sentence Pattern 5

NAME: _____

	SUBJECT	VERB (TRANSITIVE)	INDIRECT OBJECT	DIRECT OBJECT
Ex D:	*The mother*	*found*	*her son*	*an apartment.*
15.				
16.				
17.				
18.				
19.				
20.				
21.				
22.				
23.				
24.				
25.				
26.				
27.				
28.				
29.				
30.				

VARIATION C OF SENTENCE PATTERN 5

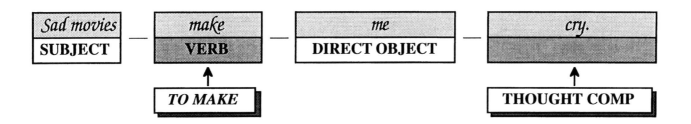

This sentence pattern is especially useful when we want to add information about the feelings or condition of the direct object.

EXAMPLES

SUBJECT	TO MAKE	DIRECT OBJECT	THOUGHT COMPLETER
Political lies	make	my friend Mark	upset.
Planning an outline	makes	English 87 students	better writers.
The clever baby	makes	her parents	proud.
Eating junk food	made	him	fat.
Exercising	makes	me	tired.

NOTE: The verb *to make* may be used in different tenses depending on appropriateness. The pronoun or noun that follows the verb *to make* is in the objective case. The thought completer adds details about the direct object.

VARIATION D OF SENTENCE PATTERN 5

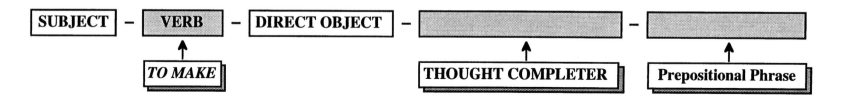

EXAMPLES

SUBJECT	*TO MAKE*	DIRECT OBJECT	THOUGHT COMPLETER	Prep Phrase
Political lies	make	my friend Mark	upset	about politicians.
Planning an outline	makes	English 87 students	better writers	in all classes.
The clever baby	makes	her parents	proud	of her.
Eating junk food	made	him	fat	around the waist.
Exercising	makes	me	feel better	in general.

> **NOTE:** The prepositional phrase at the end of the sentence adds more details to the sentence. It is **OPTIONAL** and may be added whenever appropriate.

The following pages provide practice in writing sentences according to this pattern.

NAME: _____ DATE: _____

	SUBJECT	*TO MAKE*	DIRECT OBJECT	THOUGHT COMP	Prepositional Phrase
Ex A:	Comedies	make	the audience	laugh.	
Ex B:	Hot weather	makes	people	sleepy.	
Ex C:	Political speeches	make	me	confused	about issues.
1.					
2.					
3.					
4.					
5.					
6.					
7.					
8.					
9.					
10.					
11.					
12.					
13.					
14.					

Sentence Pattern 5

NAME:

	SUBJECT	*TO MAKE*	DIRECT OBJECT	THOUGHT COMP	Prepositional Phrase
Ex D:	*Country music*	*makes*	*Mary Lee*	*homesick*	*for the Midwest.*
15.					
16.					
17.					
18.					
19.					
20.					
21.					
22.					
23.					
24.					
25.					
26.					
27.					
28.					
29.					
30.					

Sentence Pattern 5

NAME: _____   DATE: _____

	SUBJECT	*TO MAKE*	DIRECT OBJECT	THOUGHT COMP	Prepositional Phrase
Ex A:	Practice exercises	make	students	logical	in their thinking.
Ex B:	A home-cooked meal	makes	John	think	of his grandmother.
Ex C:	Rock music	makes	my head	hurt.	
1.					
2.					
3.					
4.					
5.					
6.					
7.					
8.					
9.					
10.					
11.					
12.					
13.					
14.					

NAME:

	SUBJECT	*TO MAKE*	DIRECT OBJECT	THOUGHT COMP	Prepositional Phrase
Ex D:	*Violent movies*	*make*	*Minh*	*scared*	*of the dark.*
15.					
16.					
17.					
18.					
19.					
20.					
21.					
22.					
23.					
24.					
25.					
26.					
27.					
28.					
29.					
30.					

Sentence Pattern 5

VARIATION E OF SENTENCE PATTERN 5

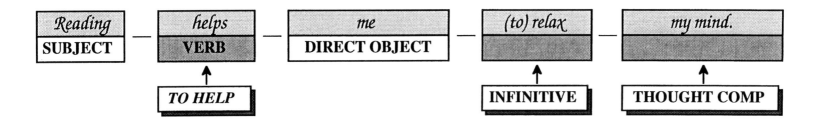

This sentence pattern helps us express the usefulness of a person or a thing.

EXAMPLES

SUBJECT	*TO HELP*	DIRECT OBJECT	INFINITIVE	THOUGHT COMPLETER
The TV	helps	me	(to) entertain	my children.
My mother	helps	me	(to) cook	dinner.
My neighbor	helps	me	(to) watch	my house.
Being sociable	helps	my mother	(to) stay	young.
Computer courses	helped	Tran	(to) find	a better job.

NOTE: The verb *to help* may be used in different tenses depending on appropriateness. Note that the verb after the direct object is an infinitive with the *to* being **OPTIONAL**.

VARIATION F OF SENTENCE PATTERN 5

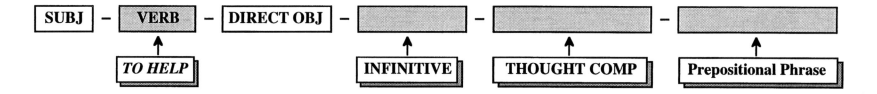

EXAMPLES

SUBJECT	*TO HELP*	DIRECT OBJECT	INFINITIVE	THOUGHT COMP	PREP PHRASE
The TV	helps	me	(to) entertain	my children	in the afternoon.
My mother	helps	me	(to) cook	dinner	in the evening.
My neighbor	helps	me	(to) watch	my house	during my vacation.
Being sociable	helps	my mother	(to) stay	young	at heart.
Computer courses	helped	Tran	(to) find	a better job	after college.

NOTE: The *to* in the infinitive may be used though it is usually omitted. The prepositional phrase in the thought completer adds more details to the sentence. It is **OPTIONAL** and may be added whenever appropriate.

The following pages provide practice in writing sentences according to this pattern.

NAME: DATE:

	SUBJECT	*TO HELP*	DIRECT OBJECT	INF	THOUGHT COMP	Prepositional Phrase
Ex A:	*The automobile*	*helps*	*people*	*get*	*to work*	*on time.*
Ex B:	*The answering machine*	*helps*	*Thomas*	*screen*	*his telephone calls*	*in the morning.*
Ex C:	*Mary's son*	*helps*	*her*	*watch*	*the store*	*in the summer.*
1.						
2.						
3.						
4.						
5.						
6.						
7.						
8.						
9.						
10.						
11.						
12.						
13.						
14.						

NAME:

SUBJECT	*TO HELP*	DIRECT OBJECT	INF	THOUGHT COMP	Prepositional Phrase
Ex D: *The carpool*	*helps*	*Mark*	*get*	*to work*	*on time.*
15.					
16.					
17.					
18.					
19.					
20.					
21.					
22.					
23.					
24.					
25.					
26.					
27.					
28.					
29.					
30.					

NAME: _____   DATE: _____

	SUBJECT	*TO HELP*	DIRECT OBJECT	INF	THOUGHT COMP	Prepositional Phrase
Ex A:	*Writing sentences*	*helps*	*the students*	*do*	*better*	*in their compositions.*
Ex B:	*Playing the violin*	*helps*	*youngsters*	*develop*	*their motor skills.*	
Ex C:	*Dining at home*	*helps*	*families*	*stay*	*together*	*as a family.*
1.						
2.						
3.						
4.						
5.						
6.						
7.						
8.						
9.						
10.						
11.						
12.						
13.						
14.						

© 1997 R. Fung

NAME:

SUBJECT	*TO HELP*	DIRECT OBJECT	INF	THOUGHT COMP	Prepositional Phrase
Ex D: *Hard work*	*helps*	*Tran*	*achieve*	*his goal*	*of a doctorate degree.*
15.					
16.					
17.					
18.					
19.					
20.					
21.					
22.					
23.					
24.					
25.					
26.					
27.					
28.					
29.					
30.					

VARIATION G OF SENTENCE PATTERN 5

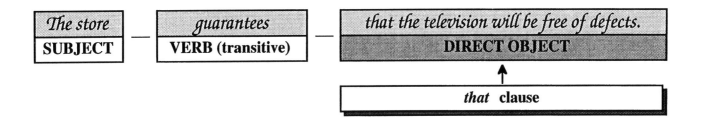

In this complex sentence, the transitive verb is followed by a *that* clause. This clause is a noun clause and substitutes for the noun in the direct object. The function of this noun clause is to expand the meaning of the sentence through the use of a *that* clause instead of a single noun as the direct object.

NOTE:	Here is a list of verbs commonly used in this sentence pattern variation.		
argue	doubt	learn	see
announce	expect	notice	sense
anticipate	fear	presume	show
ask	forget	pretend	state
believe	guarantee	regret	suggest
decide	hope	remember	swear
determine	imagine	request	think
discover	know	say	understand

VARIATION G OF SENTENCE PATTERN 5

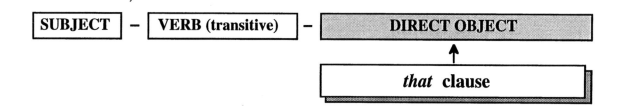

SUBJECT – VERB (transitive) – DIRECT OBJECT

↑

that clause

EXAMPLES

SUBJECT	VERB (transitive)	*that* clause
Sandra	said	*that* she would attend Sacramento State University.
Joe	announced	*that* he would quit school.
Tran	pretended	*that* he did not hear the unkind remark.
The professor	sensed	*that* the students did not understand the theory.
The store	guarantees	*that* the television will be free of defects.

NOTE: The word *that* may be omitted without changing the meaning of the sentence. When omitted, the word *that* is implied and understood. This sentence variation allows the writer to expand the meaning of the direct object. The direct object is not a single noun but a noun clause complete with subject and verb. This sentence pattern variation is a complex sentence with the *that* clause being the dependent clause.

The following pages provide practice in writing sentences according to this pattern.

NAME: _____   DATE: _____

	SUBJECT	VERB (TRANSITIVE)	*THAT* CLAUSE
Ex A:	*Many people*	*believe*	***that*** *smoking should be banned in public places.*
Ex B:	*Some people*	*argue*	***that*** *everyone should have the right to choose.*
Ex C:	*Most teenagers*	*think*	***that*** *smoking is cool.*
1.			
2.			
3.			
4.			
5.			
6.			
7.			
8.			
9.			
10.			
11.			
12.			
13.			
14.			

Sentence Pattern 5

NAME: _____

SUBJECT	VERB (TRANSITIVE)	*THAT* CLAUSE
Ex A: *Angela*	*forgot*	***that*** *she had a doctor's appointment.*
15.		
16.		
17.		
18.		
19.		
20.		
21.		
22.		
23.		
24.		
25.		
26.		
27.		
28.		
29.		
30.		

NAME: _____   DATE: _____

	SUBJECT	VERB (TRANSITIVE)	*THAT* CLAUSE
Ex A:	*Ramon*	*thinks*	***that*** *he has missed his opportunities.*
Ex B:	*Nguyen*	*senses*	***that*** *Tran is interested in a date.*
Ex C:	*Kumiko*	*pretends*	***that*** *she does not understand English.*
1.			
2.			
3.			
4.			
5.			
6.			
7.			
8.			
9.			
10.			
11.			
12.			
13.			
14.			

Sentence Pattern 5

NAME: _____

	SUBJECT	VERB (TRANSITIVE)	*THAT* CLAUSE
Ex A:	*Tom's ex-wife*	*argued*	*that* *she should have gotten the house.*
15.			
16.			
17.			
18.			
19.			
20.			
21.			
22.			
23.			
24.			
25.			
26.			
27.			
28.			
29.			
30.			

VARIATION H OF SENTENCE PATTERN 5

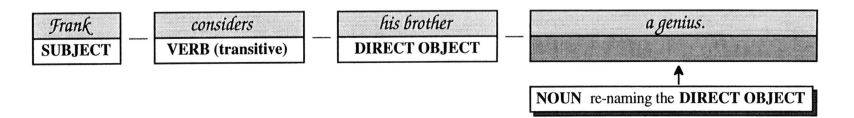

In this pattern the direct object itself is followed by a noun or a noun phrase. The function of this noun or noun phrase is to say something about the object or to act as a thought completer.

EXAMPLES

SUBJECT	VERB (transitive)	DIRECT OBJ	NOUN re-naming the DIRECT OBJECT
Tourists	call	Hong Kong	the Pearl of the Orient.
Tran	found	his sister	a changed person.
Jane's friends	call	her	a free spirit.
Madonna's music videos	made	her	a superstar.
The students	elected	John Smith	the Student Council President.

NOTE: Here is a list of verbs commonly used in this sentence pattern variation.

appoint	consider	find	make	pronounce
call	elect	label	nickname	think

© 1997 R. Fung

VARIATION I OF SENTENCE PATTERN 5

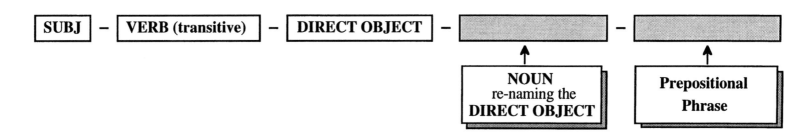

This sentence pattern variation gives the bare-bones sentence more details. The **noun** adds to the meaning of the direct object. The prepositional phrase is **OPTIONAL** and acts as a thought completer.

EXAMPLES

SUBJECT	VERB (trans)	DIRECT OBJ	NOUN re-naming the DIRECT OBJECT	Prepositional Phrase
Tourists	call	Hong Kong	the Pearl of the Orient.	
Tran	found	his sister	a changed person	after her serious illness.
Jane's friends	call	her	a free spirit.	
Madonna's music videos	made	her	a superstar.	
The students	elected	John Smith	president	of the Student Council.

The following pages provide practice in writing sentences according to this pattern.

NAME: _____   DATE: _____

	SUBJECT	VERB (TRANSITIVE)	DIRECT OBJECT	NOUN	Prepositional Phrase
Ex A:	*Tourists*	*consider*	*London traffic*	*a nightmare.*	
Ex B:	*The students*	*elected*	*Mary Smith*	*secretary*	*of the Student Council.*
Ex C:	*The children*	*called*	*their pet*	*Bambi.*	
1.					
2.					
3.					
4.					
5.					
6.					
7.					
8.					
9.					
10.					
11.					
12.					
13.					
14.					

Sentence Pattern 5

NAME:

SUBJECT	VERB (TRANSITIVE)	DIRECT OBJECT	NOUN	Prepositional Phrase
Ex D: *Tom's friends*	*nicknamed*	*him*	*Bozo.*	
15.				
16.				
17.				
18.				
19.				
20.				
21.				
22.				
23.				
24.				
25.				
26.				
27.				
28.				
29.				
30.				

NAME: _____   DATE: _____

	SUBJECT	VERB (TRANSITIVE)	DIRECT OBJECT	NOUN	Prepositional Phrase
Ex A:	*Janet*	*appointed*	*Stewart*	*the keeper*	*of the gates.*
Ex B:	*The citizens*	*pronounced*	*Lee Wai*	*the leader*	*of their country.*
Ex C:	*John's drug addiction*	*made*	*him*	*a loser*	*in life.*
1.					
2.					
3.					
4.					
5.					
6.					
7.					
8.					
9.					
10.					
11.					
12.					
13.					
14.					

NAME:

	SUBJECT	VERB (TRANSITIVE)	DIRECT OBJECT	NOUN	Prepositional Phrase
Ex D:	*The students*	*found*	*their homework*	*a challenge.*	
15.					
16.					
17.					
18.					
19.					
20.					
21.					
22.					
23.					
24.					
25.					
26.					
27.					
28.					
29.					
30.					

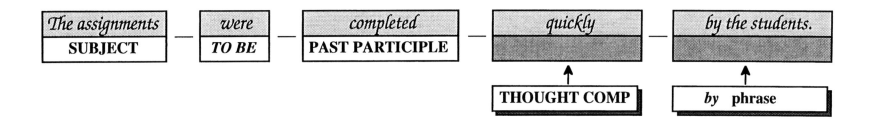

English verbs have two voices: **the active** and **the passive**. Most of the verbs you have seen in this sentence manual have been in the active voice. In the active voice, the doer of the action is the subject of the sentence, and the receiver of the action is the object. The passive voice is different. The receiver of the action becomes the subject of the verb in the passive voice while the doer of the action may be omitted or stated as the object of the preposition *by*. The passive voice is used when we want to emphasize the receiver of the action or when the doer of the action is unknown or not revealed. To form the passive voice, we use the appropriate form and tense of the verb *to be* plus the past participle of a transitive verb.

EXAMPLES

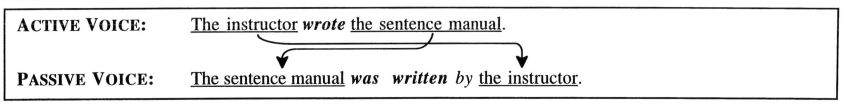

NOTE: Note that the object of the first example *sentence manual* becomes the subject in the second example, thus changing the emphasis of the sentence.

PASSIVE VOICE

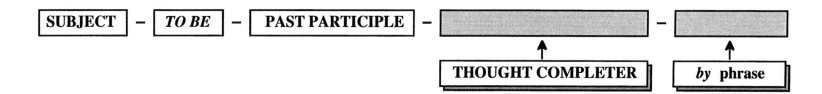

SUBJECT – *TO BE* – PAST PARTICIPLE – [THOUGHT COMPLETER] – [*by* phrase]

EXAMPLES

SUBJECT	*TO BE*	PAST PARTICIPLE of an ACTION VERB	THOUGHT COMPLETER	*by* phrase
The cheesecake	was	eaten	with ice cream.	
The chores	were	completed	quickly	by the children.
The vase	was	broken		by the little boy.
The patient	was	saved	from a heart attack	by the doctor.
The firefighters	were	alerted	about the fire	by a caller.

NOTE: Both the thought completer and the *by* phrase are **OPTIONAL**, and they may be added to the sentence whenever appropriate.

The following pages provide practice in writing sentences according to this pattern.

© 1997 R. Fung

NAME: _____ DATE: _____

	SUBJECT	*TO BE*	PAST PARTICIPLE	THOUGHT COMPLETER	*by* PHRASE
Ex A:	*The jigsaw puzzle*	*was*	*completed*		*by me.*
Ex B:	*The President*	*was*	*driven*	*to the Convention Center*	*by the chauffeur.*
Ex C:	*The car keys*	*are*	*misplaced*	*in the cabinet*	*by the child.*
1.					
2.					
3.					
4.					
5.					
6.					
7.					
8.					
9.					
10.					
11.					
12.					
13.					
14.					

Passive Voice

NAME: _____

SUBJECT	*TO BE*	PAST PARTICIPLE	THOUGHT COMPLETER	*by* PHRASE
Ex D: *The painting*	*was*	*donated*	*to the museum*	*by the late Lady Farnsworth.*
15.				
16.				
17.				
18.				
19.				
20.				
21.				
22.				
23.				
24.				
25.				
26.				
27.				
28.				
29.				
30.				

NAME: _____   DATE: _____

	SUBJECT	*TO BE*	PAST PARTICIPLE	THOUGHT COMPLETER	*by* PHRASE
Ex A:	*Tom*	*was*	*impressed*		*by the fireworks.*
Ex B:	*The baby*	*was*	*kissed*	*tenderly*	*by all the relatives.*
Ex C:	*The young boy*	*was*	*saved*	*from the fire*	*by his father.*
1.					
2.					
3.					
4.					
5.					
6.					
7.					
8.					
9.					
10.					
11.					
12.					
13.					
14.					

Passive Voice

© 1997 R. Fung

NAME:

	SUBJECT	*TO BE*	PAST PARTICIPLE	THOUGHT COMPLETER	*by* PHRASE
Ex D:	*The man*	*was*	*driven*	*to the airport*	*by taxi.*
15.					
16.					
17.					
18.					
19.					
20.					
21.					
22.					
23.					
24.					
25.					
26.					
27.					
28.					
29.					
30.					

SENTENCE PATTERN 6

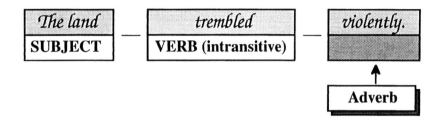

EXAMPLES

SUBJECT	VERB (intransitive)	Adverb (Optional Modifier)
The window	*cracked*	unexpectedly.
Money	*talks*.	
The lovers	*met*	secretly.

NOTE:

- The **subject** is what we are talking about. It is the actor or the performer of the action expressed by the verb.

- The **intransitive verb** is an action verb that shows the action of the subject, but the action is not transmitted elsewhere. Some verbs can be either transitive or intransitive. When they are intransitive, the action is complete in the subject and verb. There is no object. Following is a list of verbs that may be used as intransitive verbs to construct sentences in this pattern.

arrive	cheat	dream	laugh	sigh
believe	complain	happen	object	suffer
change	contribute	hesitate	rejoice	work

VARIATION OF SENTENCE PATTERN 6

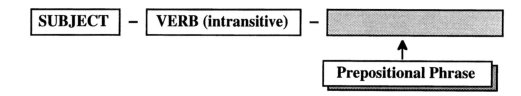

EXAMPLES

SUBJECT	VERB (intransitive)	Prepositional Phrase
The window	*cracked*	during the storm.
Money	*talks*	to most people.
The lovers	*met*	for an hour.
The First Lady	*talked*	to the teenagers.
The citizens	*sighed*	with relief.

NOTE: The **intransitive verb** is an **action verb**. The action, however, is not transmitted elsewhere. The action of the verb expresses what the subject does, and the thought is complete. Some verbs can be either transitive or intransitive. When they are intransitive, the action is complete in the subject and verb. There is no object.

The following pages provide practice in writing sentences according to this pattern.

© 1997 R. Fung

NAME: _____ DATE: _____

	SUBJECT	VERB (INTRANSITIVE)	Prepositional Phrase
Ex A:	The rabbits	hop	along the fence.
Ex B:	The monkeys	swing	from tree to tree.
Ex C:	The sun	sets	behind the hills in the evening.
1.			
2.			
3.			
4.			
5.			
6.			
7.			
8.			
9.			
10.			
11.			
12.			
13.			
14.			

Sentence Pattern 6

NAME:

SUBJECT	VERB (INTRANSITIVE)	Prepositional Phrase
Ex D: *The skunks*	*feed*	*in the ditches.*
15.		
16.		
17.		
18.		
19.		
20.		
21.		
22.		
23.		
24.		
25.		
26.		
27.		
28.		
29.		
30.		

NAME: _____   DATE: _____

	SUBJECT	VERB (INTRANSITIVE)	Prepositional Phrase
Ex A:	*Jane*	*sings*	*in the bathroom.*
Ex B:	*Minh*	*prays*	*to her ancestors.*
Ex C:	*The orphans*	*play*	*in the streets.*
1.			
2.			
3.			
4.			
5.			
6.			
7.			
8.			
9.			
10.			
11.			
12.			
13.			
14.			

Sentence Pattern 6

NAME: _____

SUBJECT	VERB (INTRANSITIVE)	Prepositional Phrase
Ex D: *The sun*	*rises*	*in the morning.*
15.		
16.		
17.		
18.		
19.		
20.		
21.		
22.		
23.		
24.		
25.		
26.		
27.		
28.		
29.		
30.		

SENTENCE COMBINING BY COORDINATION

| COMPLETE SENTENCE | , COORDINATING CONJUNCTION | COMPLETE SENTENCE |

(Note the necessary **comma**.)

This method of combining clauses is called coordination. Related sentences of equal importance are connected with a comma followed by a coordinating conjunction. The choice of the conjunction signifies the relationship of the two sentences. This kind of sentence is a compound sentence. There are seven coordinating conjunctions and can be best remembered with the memory word: **FANBOYS**.

Memory Word	Coordinating Conjunction	Meaning
Fanboys	for	cause
f **A**nboys	and	addition
fa **N**boys	nor	negative alternative
fan **B**oys	but	contrast
fanb **O**ys	or	positive alternative
fanbo **Y** s	yet	contrast
fanboy **S**	so	result

NOTE: The negative alternative *nor* needs special attention in a separate unit, but the other coordinating conjunctions *for, and, but, or, yet,* and *so* are reviewed on the following page.

© 1997 R. Fung

Coordination

COORDINATION

COMPLETE SENTENCE	, COORDINATING CONJUNCTION	COMPLETE SENTENCE

↗

(Note the necessary **comma**.)

EXAMPLES

COMPLETE SENTENCE	, coordinating conjunction (meaning)	COMPLETE SENTENCE
Brian Smith ran all the way to school	**, for** (cause)	he woke up late again.
His professor didn't like tardiness	**, and** (addition)	Brian didn't want to upset his professor.
Brian ran as fast as he could	**, but** (contrast)	he did not make it on time.
He could walk into class late	**, or** (positive alternative)	he could skip class entirely.
He knew his professor would be upset	**, yet** (contrast)	he entered the room anyway.
He listened attentively	**, so** (result)	he would not miss the lecture.

COORDINATION

Sometimes we wish to connect two complete sentences to show a pair of negative statements. This kind of connection is accomplished with a comma and the coordinating conjunction *nor*.

COMBINING SENTENCES using *NOR*

COMPLETE SENTENCE	, *NOR*	COMPLETE SENTENCE in inverted word order

(Note the necessary **comma**.)

This sentence pattern, which deals with negative alternatives, needs special attention. The first sentence is a stated negative alternative. The conjunction *nor* and the inverted order of words form the second negative alterative.

EXAMPLE

FIRST NEGATIVE ALTERNATIVE	SECOND NEGATIVE ALTERNATIVE
Mary *did not touch* her dinner	, *nor did* she *give* it to her dog.

NOTE: In the negative alternative, the auxiliary verb comes before the subject instead of after the subject. The subject *she* separates the verb phrase *did give*. The coordinating conjunction *nor* and this unusual sentence order identify the second negative alternative.

Coordination

COMBINING SENTENCES using *NOR*

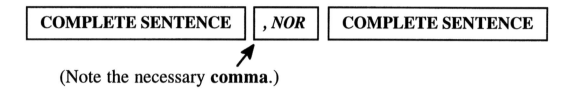

(Note the necessary **comma**.)

This pattern consists of two negative alternatives of equal importance. In this pattern the two negative alternatives are connected with a comma followed by the coordinating conjunction *nor*.

COMPLETE SENTENCE	, NOR	COMPLETE SENTENCE
Mary did not do the dishes	, nor	did she wash the laundry.
Tran would not study	, nor	would he babysit his brother.
Janet does not play the piano	, nor	does she play the guitar.
Lan could not speak French	, nor	could she speak English.
Minh will not give up	, nor	will she leave school.

NOTE: The verb phrase in the second sentence is divided by the subject. This inverted order of words works together with the conjunction *nor* to form the second negative alternative. The verb tense is consistent in both sentences.

The following pages provide practice in writing sentences with all seven coordinating conjunctions. Choose the coordinating conjunction carefully to indicate the relationship of the two sentences.

NAME: _____   DATE: _____

COMPLETE SENTENCE	, COORD CONJ	COMPLETE SENTENCE
Ex A: *Midori did not want to cook*	*, for*	*it was very late.*
Ex B: *Her stomach started growling*	*, and*	*she was beginning to feel faint.*
Ex C: *She had some money at the bank*	*, but*	*she did not have any transportation.*
1.		
2.		
3.		
4.		
5.		
6.		
7.		
8.		
9.		
10.		
11.		
12.		
13.		
14.		

Coordination

NAME: _____

COMPLETE SENTENCE	, COORD CONJ	COMPLETE SENTENCE
Ex D: *Her brother did not have any cash*	*, nor*	*did he have the car keys.*
15.		
16.		
17.		
18.		
19.		
20.		
21.		
22.		
23.		
24.		
25.		
26.		
27.		
28.		
29.		
30.		

NAME: _____   DATE: _____

COMPLETE SENTENCE	, COORD CONJ	COMPLETE SENTENCE
Ex A: *She could borrow money from her sister*	*, or*	*she could call her mother.*
Ex B: *Midori ate at McDonald's with her sister*	*, yet*	*she was hungry again after two hours.*
Ex C: *She wanted something to eat again*	*, so*	*she called her mother.*
1.		
2.		
3.		
4.		
5.		
6.		
7.		
8.		
9.		
10.		
11.		
12.		
13.		
14.		

Coordination

© 1997 R. Fung

NAME: _____

COMPLETE SENTENCE	, COORD CONJ	COMPLETE SENTENCE
Ex D: *Midori's mother could not leave work*	*, nor*	*could she see the humor in her daughter's story.*
15.		
16.		
17.		
18.		
19.		
20.		
21.		
22.		
23.		
24.		
25.		
26.		
27.		
28.		
29.		
30.		

SENTENCE COMBINING BY SUBORDINATION — INTRODUCTION

Subordination connects two clauses, and the exact relationship of the two clauses is made clear by a subordinating conjunction. When the subordinating conjunction is placed before a clause, the meaning of that clause becomes incomplete. Thus it becomes a dependent clause in a combined sentence, and it depends on the independent clause to complete its meaning. This kind of sentence is called a complex sentence. In this unit we concentrate on dependent adverb clauses. There are *many* subordinating conjunctions for dependent clauses. Following is a list of commonly used subordinating conjunctions for adverb clauses classified into four categories.

Common Subordinating Conjunctions for Adverb Clauses			
Time	**Causality**	**Contradiction**	**Condition**
after	because	although	if
before	since (meaning *because*)	even though	unless
when	as (meaning *because*)	though	
while			
until			

NOTE: Careful selection of the subordinating conjunction helps to clarify the exact relationship of the two clauses.

SUBORDINATION

The following examples show how the subordinating conjunction makes the meaning of the clause incomplete.

Subordinating Conjunction	Subject	Predicate
when	Tom	watches television
if	Joe	wins the race

The incomplete thought of the subordinate or dependent clause needs an independent clause to complete its meaning. The punctuation of the subordinate or dependent clause varies according to whether the clause appears *before* or *after* the independent clause.

Before Pattern   (Note the necessary *comma*.)

DEPENDENT CLAUSE		,	INDEPENDENT CLAUSE
When	Tom watches television	,	he forgets to eat.
If	John wins this race	,	he will retire from competitive sports.

After Pattern   (Note that there is *no comma* separating the two clauses.)

INDEPENDENT CLAUSE	DEPENDENT CLAUSE	
Tom forgets to eat	**when**	he watches television.
John will retire from competitive sports	**if**	he wins this race.

© 1997 R. Fung

SUBORDINATION — BEFORE PATTERN

When the subordinate or dependent clause appears before the independent clause, there is a comma separating the two clauses.

PATTERN

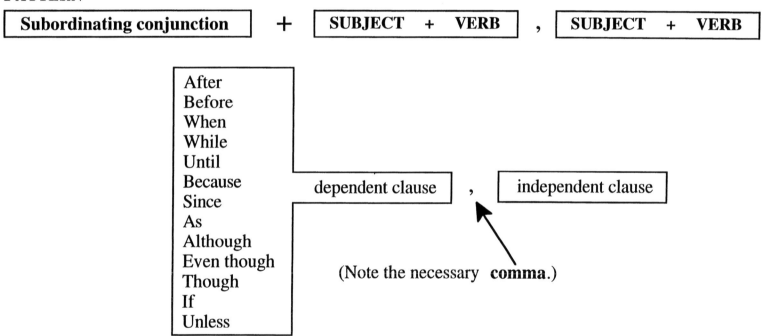

| Subordinating conjunction | **+** | SUBJECT + VERB | , | SUBJECT + VERB |

After
Before
When
While
Until
Because
Since
As
Although
Even though
Though
If
Unless

dependent clause   ,   independent clause

(Note the necessary **comma**.)

NOTE: Careful selection of the subordinating conjunction helps to clarify the exact relationship of the two clauses.

SUBORDINATION — BEFORE PATTERN

PATTERN

Subordinating conjunction	+	SUBJECT + VERB	,	SUBJECT + VERB

	DEPENDENT CLAUSE	,	INDEPENDENT CLAUSE
After	the fans picked up their tickets	,	they entered the gym.
Before	the competition began	,	the fans were talking and laughing.
When	the music started	,	a hush came over the gymnasium.
While	the competitors warmed up	,	the spectators waited patiently.
Because	all the competitors were great athletes	,	it was difficult to predict the winner.
Since	everyone performed almost flawlessly	,	even the judges had trouble making a decision.
As	it was the last competition	,	the fans were beginning to get tired.
Although	the favorite did not win	,	the fans were satisfied.
If	Tanya had not tripped	,	she would have won first place.
Unless	Yelena performed flawlessly	,	she had no hope of getting a medal.

The following pages provide practice in writing sentences according to this pattern. Choose the subordinating conjunction carefully to indicate the relationship of the two sentences.

NAME: _____   DATE: _____

	DEPENDENT CLAUSE	,	INDEPENDENT CLAUSE
Ex A: *After*	*the rain stopped*	,	*the children went out to play.*
Ex B: *Before*	*they had their picnic*	,	*they played baseball.*
Ex C: *When*	*they were hungry*	,	*they sat down to eat.*
1.			
2.			
3.			
4.			
5.			
6.			
7.			
8.			
9.			
10.			
11.			
12.			
13.			
14.			

Subordination

NAME: _____

	DEPENDENT CLAUSE	,	INDEPENDENT CLAUSE
Ex D: *Until*	*the food on the table was all gone*	,	*no one spoke.*
15.			
16.			
17.			
18.			
19.			
20.			
21.			
22.			
23.			
24.			
25.			
26.			
27.			
28.			
29.			
30.			

Subordination

NAME: _____ DATE: _____

DEPENDENT CLAUSE	,	INDEPENDENT CLAUSE
Ex A: *Because*	*they wanted to play another game*	,	*they gobbled down their sandwiches.*
Ex B: *Since*	*they forgot to pack drinks*	,	*they had to go to the store.*
Ex C: *Although*	*they played another game*	,	*they did not want to go home.*
1.			
2.			
3.			
4.			
5.			
6.			
7.			
8.			
9.			
10.			
11.			
12.			
13.			
14.			

NAME: _____

DEPENDENT CLAUSE		,	INDEPENDENT CLAUSE
Ex D: *If*	*they had stayed at the park*	*,*	*their parents would have grounded them.*
15.			
16.			
17.			
18.			
19.			
20.			
21.			
22.			
23.			
24.			
25.			
26.			
27.			
28.			
29.			
30.			

SUBORDINATION — AFTER PATTERN

When the subordinate or dependent clause appears after the independent clause, there is **no comma** separating the two clauses.

PATTERN

| SUBJECT + VERB | + | subordinating conjunction | + | SUBJECT + VERB |

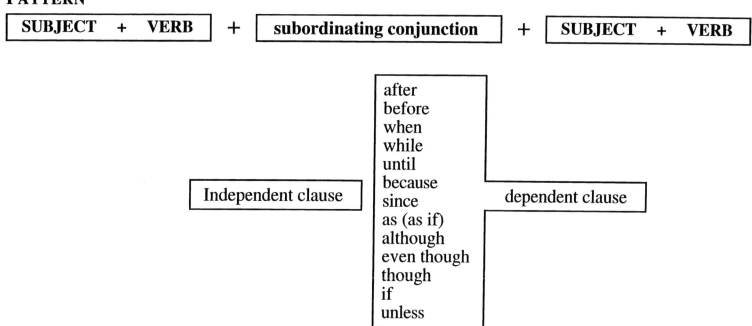

Independent clause

after
before
when
while
until
because
since
as (as if)
although
even though
though
if
unless

dependent clause

(Note that there is **no comma** separating the two clauses.)

| **NOTE:** | Careful selection of the subordinating conjunction helps to clarify the exact relationship of the two clauses. |

SUBORDINATION — AFTER PATTERN

PATTERN

| SUBJECT + VERB | + | subordinating conjunction | + | SUBJECT + VERB |

(Note that there is *no comma* separating the two clauses.)

INDEPENDENT CLAUSE		DEPENDENT CLAUSE
The fans entered the gym	**after**	they picked up their tickets.
The fans were talking and laughing	**before**	the competition began.
A hush came over the gymnasium	**when**	the music started.
The spectators waited patiently	**while**	the competitors warmed up.
It was difficult to predict the winner	**because**	all the competitors were great athletes.
Even the judges had trouble making a decision	**since**	everyone performed almost flawlessly.
The fans were beginning to get tired	**as**	it was the last competition.
The fans were satisfied	**although**	the favorite did not win.
Tanya would have won first place	**if**	she had not tripped.
Yelena had no hope of getting a medal	**unless**	she performed flawlessly.

The following pages provide practice in writing sentences according to this pattern. Choose the subordinating conjunction carefully to indicate the relationship of the two sentences.

© 1997 R. Fung

NAME: _____   DATE: _____

INDEPENDENT CLAUSE		DEPENDENT CLAUSE
Ex A: *Tom was dead tired*	*after*	*he played in the park.*
Ex B: *He had to clean up*	*before*	*he could sit down to eat.*
Ex C: *He was all washed and tidy*	*when*	*dinner was served.*
1.		
2.		
3.		
4.		
5.		
6.		
7.		
8.		
9.		
10.		
11.		
12.		
13.		
14.		

© 1997 R. Fung

NAME: _____

INDEPENDENT CLAUSE		DEPENDENT CLAUSE
Ex D: *He ate dinner*	*while*	*his dog waited to go out.*
15.		
16.		
17.		
18.		
19.		
20.		
21.		
22.		
23.		
24.		
25.		
26.		
27.		
28.		
29.		
30.		

NAME: _____   DATE: _____

	INDEPENDENT CLAUSE			DEPENDENT CLAUSE
Ex A:	*The dog was anxious to go outside*	*because*		*it had been cooped up all day.*
Ex B:	*Tom took the dog for a walk*	*although*		*he wanted to rest.*
Ex C:	*The dog would have been restless*	*if*		*it did not get its daily walk.*
1.				
2.				
3.				
4.				
5.				
6.				
7.				
8.				
9.				
10.				
11.				
12.				
13.				
14.				

NAME: _____

INDEPENDENT CLAUSE	DEPENDENT CLAUSE	
Ex D: *Tom does not neglect his chores*	*unless*	*he is sick.*
15.		
16.		
17.		
18.		
19.		
20.		
21.		
22.		
23.		
24.		
25.		
26.		
27.		
28.		
29.		
30.		

DEPENDENT ADJECTIVE CLAUSES — NON ESSENTIAL

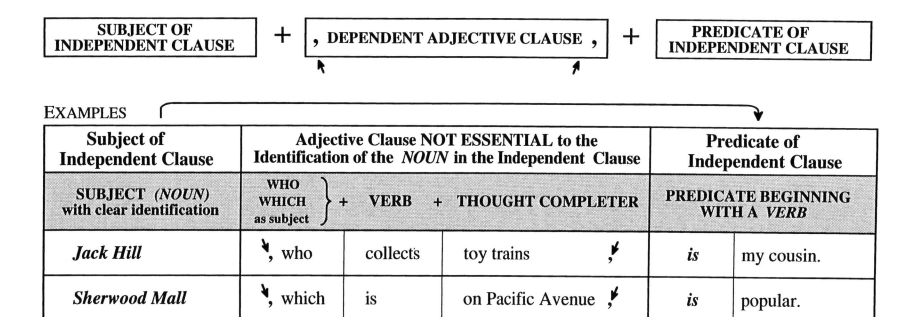

| SUBJECT OF INDEPENDENT CLAUSE | + | , DEPENDENT ADJECTIVE CLAUSE , | + | PREDICATE OF INDEPENDENT CLAUSE |

EXAMPLES

Subject of Independent Clause	Adjective Clause NOT ESSENTIAL to the Identification of the *NOUN* in the Independent Clause			Predicate of Independent Clause	
SUBJECT *(NOUN)* with clear identification	WHO WHICH as subject } +	VERB	+ THOUGHT COMPLETER	PREDICATE BEGINNING WITH A *VERB*	
Jack Hill	, who	collects	toy trains	*is*	my cousin.
Sherwood Mall	, which	is	on Pacific Avenue	*is*	popular.

NOTE: In this pattern a set of commas is necessary to set off the adjective clause. Because the subject of the independent clause is specific and is already clearly identified, the adjective clause that modifies it is **NOT ESSENTIAL** to its identification. In this case, the adjective clause is set off by commas as indicated by the arrows. *Who* is used to refer to specific people that do not need further identification. *Which* is used to refer to specific things that do not need further identification. In this pattern *who* and *which* may NOT be replaced by the relative pronoun *that*.

Adjective Clause

DEPENDENT ADJECTIVE CLAUSES — NON ESSENTIAL

| SUBJECT OF INDEPENDENT CLAUSE | **+** | , DEPENDENT ADJECTIVE CLAUSE , | **+** | PREDICATE OF INDEPENDENT CLAUSE |

EXAMPLES

Subject of Independent Clause	Adjective Clause NOT ESSENTIAL to the Identification of the *NOUN* in the Independent Clause			Predicate of Independent Clause	
SUBJECT *(NOUN)* with clear identification	WHO WHICH as subject +	VERB +	THOUGHT COMPLETER	PREDICATE BEGINNING WITH A *VERB*	
My father	, who	trades	with the French	*speaks*	three languages.
Ice hockey	, which	is	popular in Canada	*is*	a violent game.
See's Candies	, which	are	sold in California	*are*	very rich.

NOTE: In this pattern a set of commas is necessary to set off the adjective clause. Because the subject of the independent clause is specific and is already clearly identified, the adjective clause that modifies it is **NOT ESSENTIAL** to its identification. In this case, the adjective clause is set off by commas as indicated by the arrows.

The following pages provide practice in writing sentences according to this pattern.

© 1997 R. Fung

NAME: _____   DATE: _____

SUBJ (*NOUN*) with clear identification	*,WHO/WHICH* + VERB +		T C ,	PREDICATE
Ex A: *My grandfather*	*, who*	*died*	*in WW II,*	*was a decorated soldier.*
Ex B: *Weberstown Mall*	*, which*	*was built*	*thirty years ago,*	*was remodeled recently.*
Ex C: *Mariko Morita*	*, who*	*is*	*from Japan,*	*likes the United States.*
1.				
2.				
3.				
4.				
5.				
6.				
7.				
8.				
9.				
10.				
11.				
12.				
13.				
14.				

Adjective Clause

SUBJ (NOUN) with clear identification	,WHO/WHICH +	VERB +	T C ,	PREDICATE
Ex D: *The Macintosh computer*	*,which*	*is*	*user-friendly,*	*has dominated high schools.*
15.				
16.				
17.				
18.				
19.				
20.				
21.				
22.				
23.				
24.				
25.				
26.				
27.				
28.				
29.				
30.				

NAME: DATE:

NAME: _____   DATE: _____

SUBJ *(NOUN)* with clear identification	,*WHO/WHICH* + VERB +		T C ,	PREDICATE
Ex A: *My boss*	, *who*	*is*	*very pushy,*	*disapproves of my work.*
Ex B: *Meg's only daughter*	, *who*	*lives*	*in L.A.,*	*loves the mild winters.*
Ex C: *Bing and Milton*	, *who*	*own*	*a restaurant,*	*can't get along.*
1.				
2.				
3.				
4.				
5.				
6.				
7.				
8.				
9.				
10.				
11.				
12.				
13.				
14.				

Adjective Clause

NAME:	DATE:			
SUB *(NOUN)* with clear identification	*,WHO/WHICH* + VERB +		T C ,	PREDICATE
Ex D: *The Phantom of the Opera*	*,which*	*is*	*a musical,*	*has many fans.*
15.				
16.				
17.				
18.				
19.				
20.				
21.				
22.				
23.				
24.				
25.				
26.				
27.				
28.				
29.				
30.				

DEPENDENT ADJECTIVE CLAUSES — ESSENTIAL

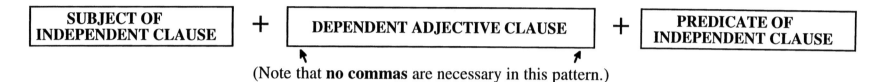

SUBJECT OF INDEPENDENT CLAUSE	+	DEPENDENT ADJECTIVE CLAUSE	+	PREDICATE OF INDEPENDENT CLAUSE

(Note that **no commas** are necessary in this pattern.)

EXAMPLES

Subject of Independent Clause	Adjective Clause ESSENTIAL to the Identification of the *NOUN* in the Independent Clause			Predicate of Independent Clause
SUBJECT *(NOUN)* that is non-specific and needs identification	WHO THAT as subject	+ VERB	+ THOUGHT COMPLETER	PREDICATE BEGINNING WITH A *VERB*
The professor	who/that	teaches	physics	*is* very friendly.
The book	that	was given	to me by my mother	*is sitting* on the shelf.

NOTE: In this pattern, **no commas** are used to set off the adjective clause. Because the subject of the independent clause is non-specific and needs to be identified, the adjective clause that modifies it is **ESSENTIAL** to its identification. In this case, the adjective clause is **not** separated from the independent clause. ***Who*** and ***that*** are used with non-specific nouns referring to people that need further identification. ***That*** is used with non-specific nouns referring to things that need further identification. Although theoretically ***that*** and ***which*** are interchangeable when they refer to non-specific things that need further identification, most writers prefer to use ***that*** for stylistic reasons.

Adjective Clause

The following pages provide practice in writing sentences according to this pattern.

NAME: DATE:

SUBJ (*NOUN*) that is non-specific	*WHO/THAT* +	VERB +	T C	PREDICATE
Ex A: *Students*	*who*	*arrive*	*late*	*often miss their tests.*
Ex B: *Children*	*that*	*play*	*video games*	*have good coordination.*
Ex C: *The piano*	*that*	*sits*	*in the study*	*is an antique.*
1.				
2.				
3.				
4.				
5.				
6.				
7.				
8.				
9.				
10.				
11.				
12.				
13.				
14.				

Adjective Clause

NAME: _____

SUBJ (*NOUN*) that is non-specific	*WHO/THAT* + VERB + T C			PREDICATE
Ex D: *Animals*	*that*	*prey*	*on other animals*	*may be dangerous.*
15.				
16.				
17.				
18.				
19.				
20.				
21.				
22.				
23.				
24.				
25.				
26.				
27.				
28.				
29.				
30.				

NAME: _____   DATE: _____

SUBJ (*NOUN*) that is non-specific	*WHO/THAT* +	VERB +	T C	PREDICATE
Ex A: *People*	*who*	*learn*	*to fly*	*gain confidence.*
Ex B: *Sports fans*	*who*	*enjoy*	*hockey*	*enjoy the playoffs.*
Ex C: *The car*	*that*	*had*	*the best mileage*	*won the prize.*
1.				
2.				
3.				
4.				
5.				
6.				
7.				
8.				
9.				
10.				
11.				
12.				
13.				
14.				

Adjective Clause

© 1997 R. Fung

NAME: _____

SUBJ (*NOUN*) that is non-specific	*WHO/THAT* + VERB + T C			PREDICATE
Ex D: *People*	*who*	*think*	*only of money*	*are foolish.*
15.				
16.				
17.				
18.				
19.				
20.				
21.				
22.				
23.				
24.				
25.				
26.				
27.				
28.				
29.				
30.				

DEPENDENT ADJECTIVE CLAUSES — NON ESSENTIAL

| SUBJECT OF INDEPENDENT CLAUSE | + | , DEPENDENT ADJECTIVE CLAUSE , | + | PREDICATE OF INDEPENDENT CLAUSE |

Adjective Clause

EXAMPLES

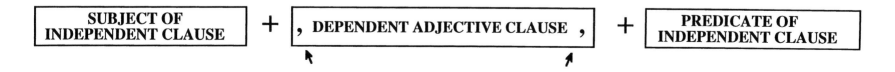

Subject of Independent Clause	Adjective Clause NOT ESSENTIAL to the Identification of the *NOUN* in the Independent Clause				Predicate of Independent Clause	
SUBJECT *(NOUN)* with clear identification	WHOM WHICH as object } +	SUBJECT +	VERB +	THOUGHT COMPLETER	PREDICATE BEGINNING WITH A *VERB*	
Yoko Morita	, whom	I	met	yesterday,	*is*	from Japan.
Florida	, which	tourists	enjoy	visiting	*has*	plenty of sunshine.

> **NOTE:** In this pattern a set of commas is necessary to set off the adjective clause. Because the subject of the independent clause is specific and is already clearly identified, the adjective clause that modifies it is **NOT ESSENTIAL** to its identification. In this case, the adjective clause is set off by commas as indicated by the arrows. **Whom** and **which** in the examples are used to refer to specific nouns that do not need further identification, and in this pattern they may **NOT** be replaced by the relative pronoun **that**.

DEPENDENT ADJECTIVE CLAUSES — NON ESSENTIAL

SUBJECT OF INDEPENDENT CLAUSE	+	, DEPENDENT ADJECTIVE CLAUSE ,	+	PREDICATE OF INDEPENDENT CLAUSE

EXAMPLES

Subject of Independent Clause	Adjective Clause NOT ESSENTIAL to the Identification of the *NOUN* in the Independent Clause				Predicate of Independent Clause	
SUBJECT *(NOUN)* with clear identification	WHOM WHICH as object	+ SUBJECT +	VERB +	THOUGHT COMPLETER	PREDICATE BEGINNING WITH A *VERB*	
Gone With the Wind	, which	most women	like	to read	*is*	also a movie.
Professor Pike	, whom	everyone	likes		*has retired*	from teaching.
Godfather II	, which	people	like	to watch	*is*	popular worldwide.

NOTE: In this pattern a set of commas is necessary to set off the adjective clause. Because the subject of the independent clause is specific and is already clearly identified, the adjective clause that modifies it is **NOT ESSENTIAL** to its identification.

The following pages provide practice in writing sentences according to this pattern.

NAME: DATE:

SUBJ (*NOUN*) with clear identification	,*WHOM/WHICH* + SUBJ + VERB + T C ,				PREDICATE
Ex A: *Judy Koseki*	, *whom*	*everybody*	*likes ,*		*is from Hawaii.*
Ex B: *Hawaii*	, *which*	*tourists*	*like*	*to visit ,*	*is enchanting.*
Ex C: *Bruce Lee*	, *whom*	*young boys*	*admire ,*		*died young.*
1.					
2.					
3.					
4.					
5.					
6.					
7.					
8.					
9.					
10.					
11.					
12.					
13.					
14.					

Adjective Clause

NAME: _____

SUBJ (*NOUN*) with clear identification	,*WHOM/WHICH* + SUBJ + VERB + T C ,				PREDICATE
Ex D: *The King of Rock*	*, whom*	*teenagers*	*adore ,*		*died tragically.*
15.					
16.					
17.					
18.					
19.					
20.					
21.					
22.					
23.					
24.					
25.					
26.					
27.					
28.					
29.					
30.					

NAME: DATE:

SUBJ *(NOUN)* with clear identification	,*WHOM/WHICH* + SUBJ + VERB + T C ,				PREDICATE
Ex A: *The Queen Mary*	, *which*	*many people*	*enjoy*	*visiting,*	*is in Long Beach.*
Ex B: *The Museum of Modern Art*	, *which*	*we*	*like*	*to visit,*	*is impressive.*
Ex C: *Susan, my cousin*	, *whom*	*I*	*find*	*pleasant,*	*has beautiful eyes.*
1.					
2.					
3.					
4.					
5.					
6.					
7.					
8.					
9.					
10.					
11.					
12.					
13.					
14.					

Adjective Clause

NAME: _____

SUBJ (*NOUN*) with clear identification	,*WHOM/WHICH* + SUBJ + VERB + T C ,				PREDICATE
Ex D: *Joe DiMaggio*	*, whom*	*sports fans*	*admire*	*immensely ,*	*married Marilyn Monroe.*
15.					
16.					
17.					
18.					
19.					
20.					
21.					
22.					
23.					
24.					
25.					
26.					
27.					
28.					
29.					
30.					

DEPENDENT ADJECTIVE CLAUSES — ESSENTIAL

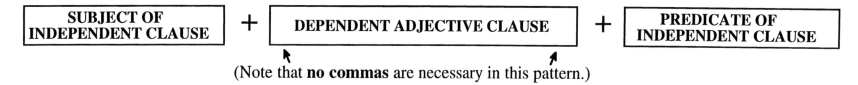

| SUBJECT OF INDEPENDENT CLAUSE | + | DEPENDENT ADJECTIVE CLAUSE | + | PREDICATE OF INDEPENDENT CLAUSE |

(Note that **no commas** are necessary in this pattern.)

EXAMPLES

Subject of Independent Clause	Adjective Clause ESSENTIAL to the Identification of the *NOUN* in the Independent Clause				Predicate of Independent Clause	
SUBJECT *(NOUN)* that is non-specific and needs identification	WHOM THAT as object } + SUBJECT + VERB +			THOUGHT COMPLETER	PREDICATE BEGINNING WITH A *VERB*	
The man	whom/that	I	met	last week	*is*	a pianist.
The book	that	Minh	bought	yesterday	*made*	a good gift.

NOTE: In this pattern, **no commas** are used to set off the adjective clause. Because the subject of the independent clause is non-specific and needs to be identified, the adjective clause that modifies it is **ESSENTIAL** to its identification. In this case, the adjective clause is **not** separated from the independent clause. *Whom* and *that* are used with non-specific nouns referring to people that need further identification. *That* is used with non-specific nouns referring to things that need further identification. Although theoretically *that* and *which* are interchangeable when they refer to non-specific things that need further identification, most writers prefer to use *that* for stylistic reasons.

Adjective Clause

DEPENDENT ADJECTIVE CLAUSES — ESSENTIAL

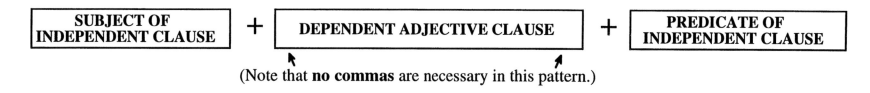

(Note that **no commas** are necessary in this pattern.)

EXAMPLES

Subject of Independent Clause	Adjective Clause ESSENTIAL to the Identification of the *NOUN* in the Independent Clause				Predicate of Independent Clause	
SUBJECT *(NOUN)* that is non-specific and needs identification	WHOM THAT *as object* +	SUBJECT +	VERB +	THOUGHT COMPLETER	PREDICATE BEGINNING WITH A *VERB*	
The painting	that	Tom	finished	for his brother	*looks*	professional.
The student	whom/that	everybody	likes		*is*	from China.
The pen	that	Judy	used	in class	*was*	a free gift.

NOTE: In this pattern, **no commas** are used to set off the adjective clause. Because the subject of the independent clause is non-specific and needs to be identified, the adjective clause that modifies it is **ESSENTIAL** to its identification. In this case, the adjective clause is **not** separated from the independent clause.

The following pages provide practice in writing sentences according to this pattern.

NAME:				DATE:	
SUBJ *(NOUN)* that is non-specific	*WHOM/THAT*	+ SUBJ	+ VERB	+ T C	PREDICATE
Ex A: *The beautiful girl*	*whom*	*Tom*	*met*	*at the party*	*speaks three languages.*
Ex A: *The teacher*	*that*	*students*	*prefer*		*is very strict.*
Ex A: *The compositions*	*that*	*teachers*	*dread*	*to read*	*have many errors.*
1.					
2.					
3.					
4.					
5.					
6.					
7.					
8.					
9.					
10.					
11.					
12.					
13.					
14.					

Adjective Clause

NAME:

SUBJ *(NOUN)* that is non-specific	WHOM/THAT	+ SUBJ +	VERB +	T C	PREDICATE
Ex D: *The weather*	*that*	*forecasters*	*failed*	*to predict*	*was unbearable.*
15.					
16.					
17.					
18.					
19.					
20.					
21.					
22.					
23.					
24.					
25.					
26.					
27.					
28.					
29.					
30.					

NAME: DATE:

SUBJ *(NOUN)* that is non-specific	*WHOM/THAT*	+ SUBJ	+ VERB	+ T C	PREDICATE
Ex A: *The models*	*whom*	*we*	*painted*	*in class*	*were pretty.*
Ex A: *The music*	*that*	*Ellen*	*heard*	*in the elevator*	*sounded familiar.*
Ex A: *The art show*	*that*	*I*	*saw*	*in San Francisco*	*made me sad.*
1.					
2.					
3.					
4.					
5.					
6.					
7.					
8.					
9.					
10.					
11.					
12.					
13.					
14.					

Adjective Clause

NAME: _____

SUBJ (*NOUN*) that is non-specific	*WHOM/THAT*	+ SUBJ +	VERB +	T C	PREDICATE
Ex D: *The floods*	*that*	*we*	*had*	*in January*	*were followed by a drought.*
15.					
16.					
17.					
18.					
19.					
20.					
21.					
22.					
23.					
24.					
25.					
26.					
27.					
28.					
29.					
30.					

RECAP

Patterns for Success, Book Four, concludes my four-volume review of some commonly used English sentence patterns and their variations. We have studied basic patterns, their variations, and methods of sentence expansion — coordination and subordination. Through the four workbooks, we have progressed from simple to more complex structures. Mastery of these patterns will bring a new fluency to both speaking and writing, and this fluency will provide a sound basis for moving on to mainstream college studies. Here is a recap of what we have studied in ***Patterns for Success, Book Four***.

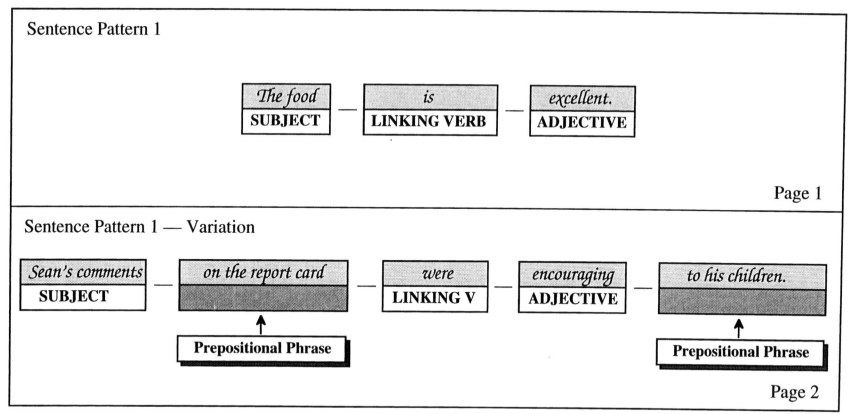

Sentence Pattern 1

| *The food* | | *is* | | *excellent.* |
| **SUBJECT** | | **LINKING VERB** | | **ADJECTIVE** |

Page 1

Sentence Pattern 1 — Variation

Sean's comments	*on the report card*	*were*	*encouraging*	*to his children.*
SUBJECT		**LINKING V**	**ADJECTIVE**	
	Prepositional Phrase			**Prepositional Phrase**

Page 2

Recap

RECAP

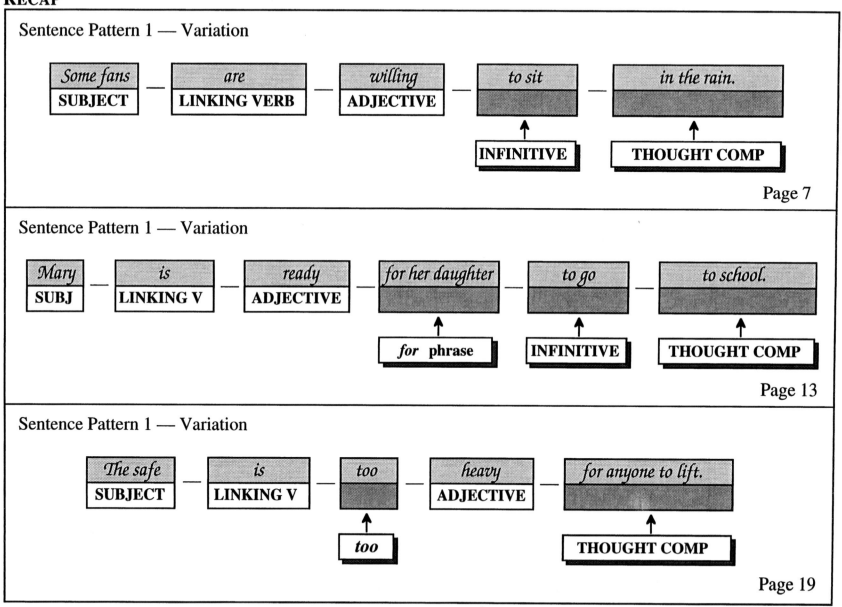

Sentence Pattern 1 — Variation

| *Some fans* | *are* | *willing* | *to sit* | *in the rain.* |
| SUBJECT | LINKING VERB | ADJECTIVE | INFINITIVE | THOUGHT COMP |

Page 7

Sentence Pattern 1 — Variation

| *Mary* | *is* | *ready* | *for her daughter* | *to go* | *to school.* |
| SUBJ | LINKING V | ADJECTIVE | *for* phrase | INFINITIVE | THOUGHT COMP |

Page 13

Sentence Pattern 1 — Variation

| *The safe* | *is* | *too* | *heavy* | *for anyone to lift.* |
| SUBJECT | LINKING V | *too* | ADJECTIVE | THOUGHT COMP |

Page 19

Sentence Pattern 1 — Variation

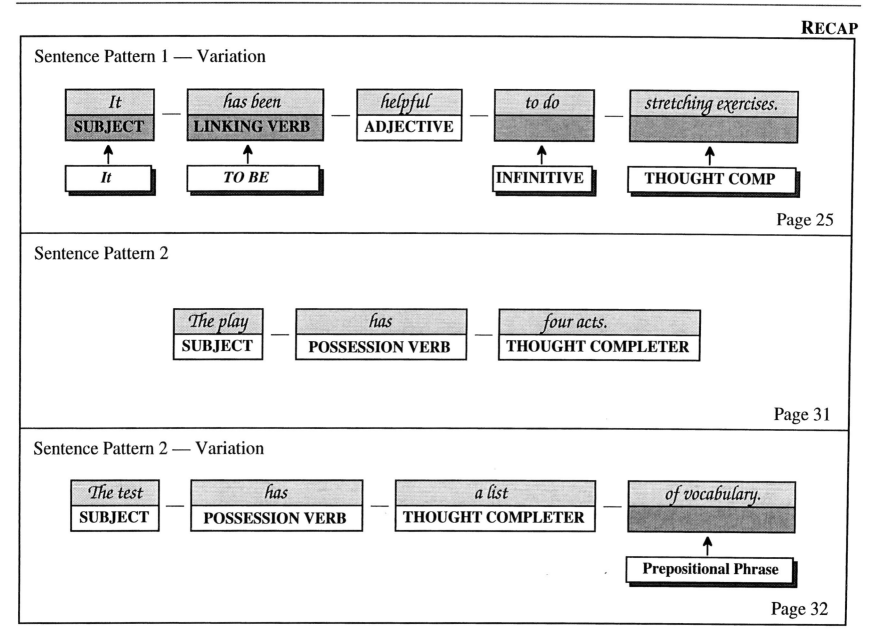

Page 25

Sentence Pattern 2

Page 31

Sentence Pattern 2 — Variation

Page 32

Recap

RECAP

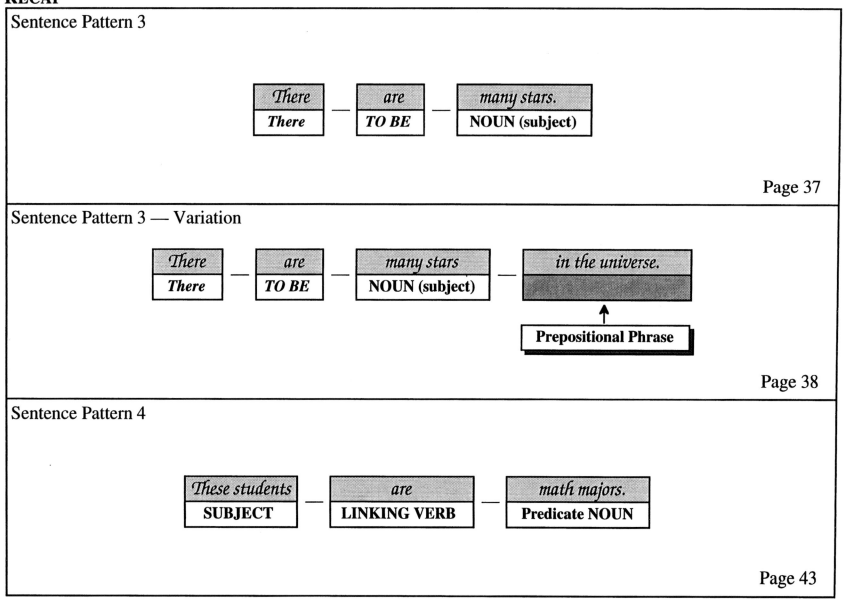

Sentence Pattern 3

There	—	are	—	many stars.
There		*TO BE*		**NOUN (subject)**

Page 37

Sentence Pattern 3 — Variation

There	—	are	—	many stars	—	in the universe.
There		*TO BE*		**NOUN (subject)**		

Prepositional Phrase

Page 38

Sentence Pattern 4

These students	—	are	—	math majors.
SUBJECT		**LINKING VERB**		**Predicate NOUN**

Page 43

RECAP

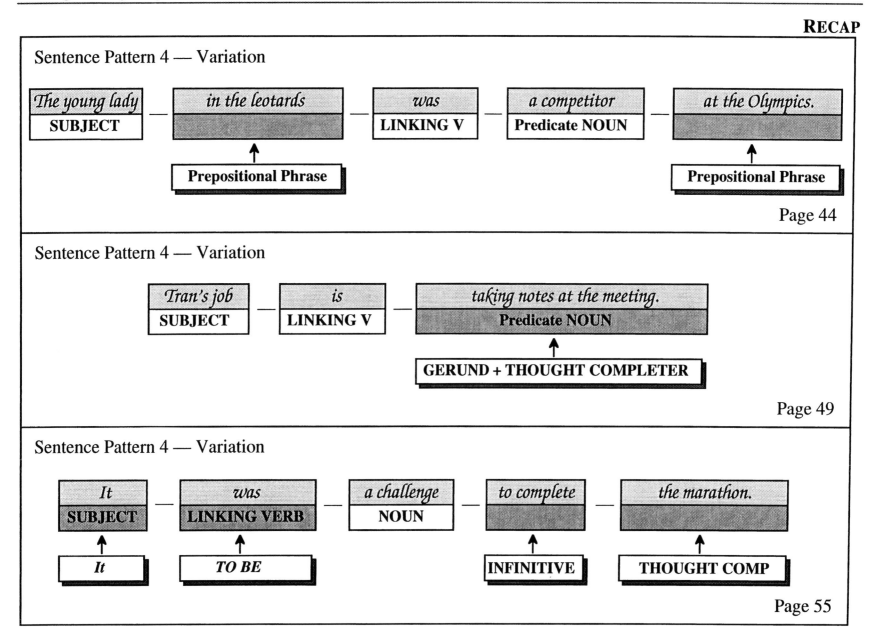

Sentence Pattern 4 — Variation

The young lady	in the leotards	was	a competitor	at the Olympics.
SUBJECT		LINKING V	Predicate NOUN	

Prepositional Phrase

Prepositional Phrase

Page 44

Sentence Pattern 4 — Variation

Tran's job	is	taking notes at the meeting.
SUBJECT	LINKING V	Predicate NOUN

GERUND + THOUGHT COMPLETER

Page 49

Sentence Pattern 4 — Variation

It	was	a challenge	to complete	the marathon.
SUBJECT	LINKING VERB	NOUN		

It

TO BE

INFINITIVE

THOUGHT COMP

Page 55

Recap

RECAP

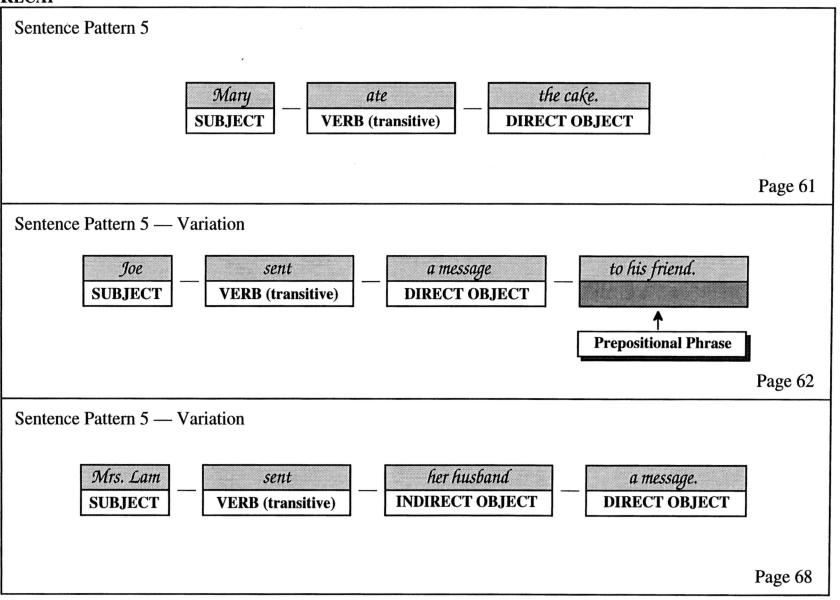

Sentence Pattern 5

| Mary | ate | the cake. |
| SUBJECT | VERB (transitive) | DIRECT OBJECT |

Page 61

Sentence Pattern 5 — Variation

| Joe | sent | a message | to his friend. |
| SUBJECT | VERB (transitive) | DIRECT OBJECT | |

↑
Prepositional Phrase

Page 62

Sentence Pattern 5 — Variation

| Mrs. Lam | sent | her husband | a message. |
| SUBJECT | VERB (transitive) | INDIRECT OBJECT | DIRECT OBJECT |

Page 68

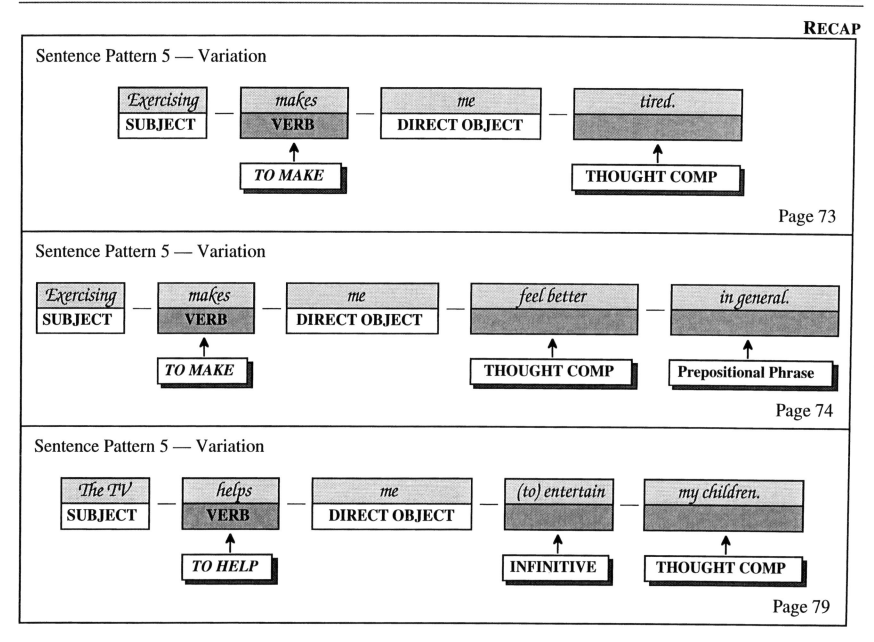

Sentence Pattern 5 — Variation

Exercising	*makes*	*me*	*tired.*
SUBJECT	VERB	DIRECT OBJECT	

TO MAKE → VERB

THOUGHT COMP → tired.

Page 73

Sentence Pattern 5 — Variation

Exercising	*makes*	*me*	*feel better*	*in general.*
SUBJECT	VERB	DIRECT OBJECT		

TO MAKE → VERB

THOUGHT COMP → feel better

Prepositional Phrase → in general.

Page 74

Sentence Pattern 5 — Variation

The TV	*helps*	*me*	*(to) entertain*	*my children.*
SUBJECT	VERB	DIRECT OBJECT		

TO HELP → VERB

INFINITIVE → (to) entertain

THOUGHT COMP → my children.

Page 79

Recap

© 1997 R. Fung

RECAP

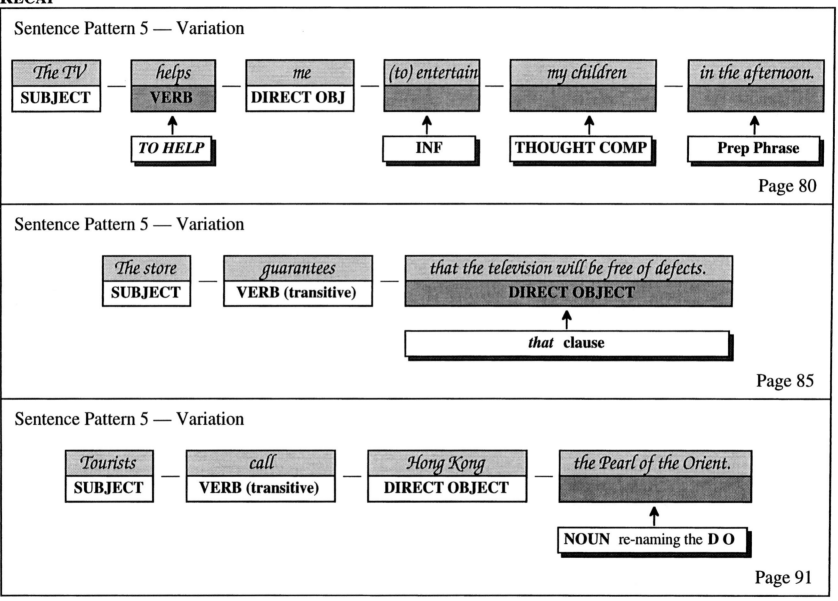

Sentence Pattern 5 — Variation

| The TV | helps | me | (to) entertain | my children | in the afternoon. |
| SUBJECT | VERB | DIRECT OBJ | | | |

TO HELP → VERB

INF → (to) entertain

THOUGHT COMP → my children

Prep Phrase → in the afternoon.

Page 80

Sentence Pattern 5 — Variation

| The store | guarantees | that the television will be free of defects. |
| SUBJECT | VERB (transitive) | DIRECT OBJECT |

that clause

Page 85

Sentence Pattern 5 — Variation

| Tourists | call | Hong Kong | the Pearl of the Orient. |
| SUBJECT | VERB (transitive) | DIRECT OBJECT | |

NOUN re-naming the D O

Page 91

RECAP

Sentence Pattern 5 — Variation

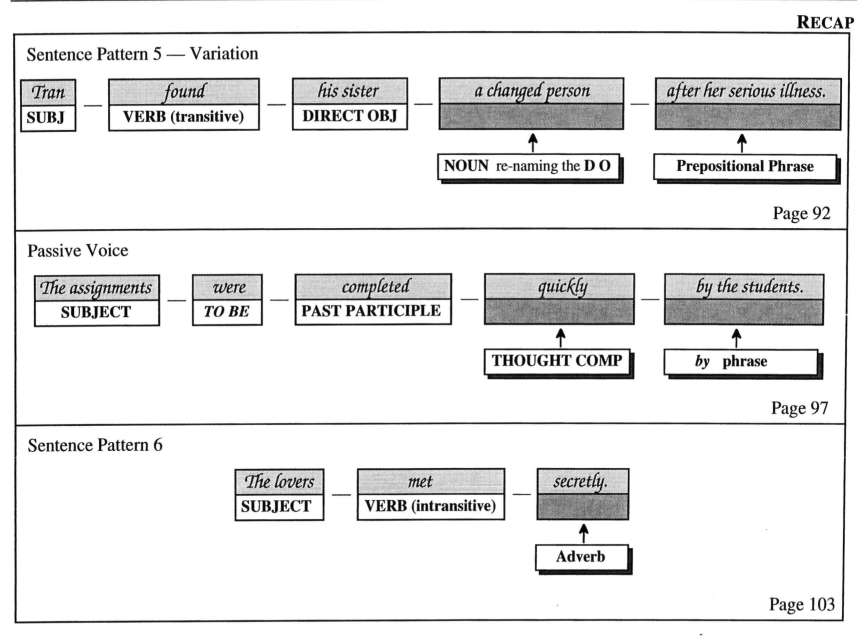

Tran	*found*	*his sister*	*a changed person*	*after her serious illness.*
SUBJ	**VERB (transitive)**	**DIRECT OBJ**		

NOUN re-naming the **D O**

Prepositional Phrase

Page 92

Passive Voice

The assignments	*were*	*completed*	*quickly*	*by the students.*
SUBJECT	*TO BE*	**PAST PARTICIPLE**		

THOUGHT COMP

by phrase

Page 97

Sentence Pattern 6

The lovers	*met*	*secretly.*
SUBJECT	**VERB (intransitive)**	

Adverb

Page 103

Recap

© 1997 R. Fung

RECAP

Sentence Pattern 6 — Variation

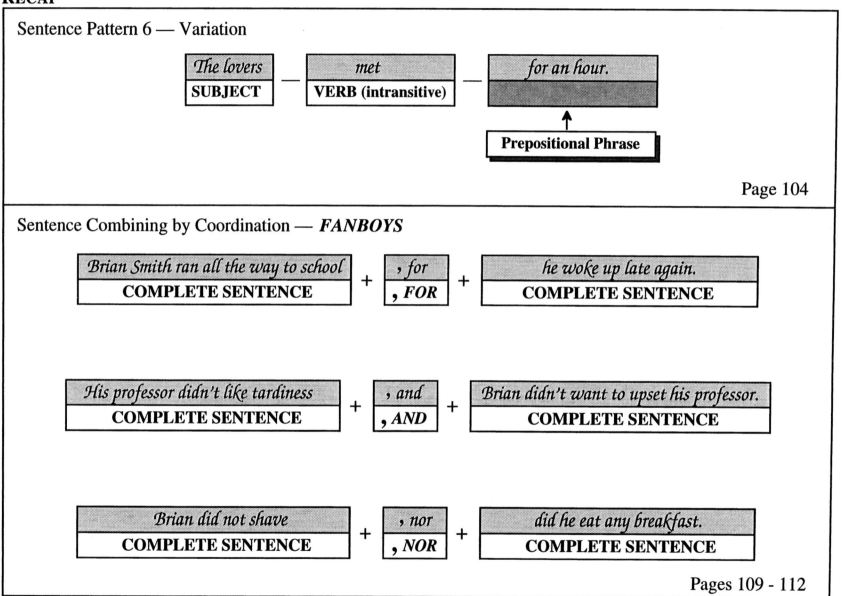

Page 104

Sentence Combining by Coordination — *FANBOYS*

Pages 109 - 112

Sentence Combining by Coordination — *FANBOYS*   (cont'd)

Brian ran as fast as he could	+	*, but*	+	*he did not make it on time.*
COMPLETE SENTENCE		**, BUT**		**COMPLETE SENTENCE**

He could walk into class late	+	*, or*	+	*he could skip class entirely.*
COMPLETE SENTENCE		**, OR**		**COMPLETE SENTENCE**

He knew his professor would be upset	+	*, yet*	+	*he entered the room anyway.*
COMPLETE SENTENCE		**, YET**		**COMPLETE SENTENCE**

He listened attentively	+	*, so*	+	*he would not miss the lecture.*
COMPLETE SENTENCE		**, SO**		**COMPLETE SENTENCE**

Pages 109 - 112

Recap

RECAP

Sentence Combining by Subordination — Before Pattern

Because all the competitors were great athletes	+	,	+	*it was difficult to predict the winner.*
DEPENDENT CLAUSE		,		**INDEPENDENT CLAUSE**

Page 119

Sentence Combining by Subordination — After Pattern

It was difficult to predict the winner	+	*because all the competitors were great athletes.*
INDEPENDENT CLAUSE		**DEPENDENT CLAUSE**

Page 125

Dependent Adjective Clauses — Non Essential

My father	+	*, who trades with the French ,*	+	*speaks three languages.*
SUBJ OF IND CLAUSE		**, DEP ADJ CLAUSE ,**		**PREDICATE OF IND CLAUSE**

Page 131

Dependent Adjective Clauses — Essential

Birds	+	*that live in the tropics*	+	*do not need to migrate.*
SUBJ OF IND CLAUSE		**DEP ADJ CLAUSE**		**PREDICATE OF IND CLAUSE**

Page 137

Dependent Adjective Clause — Non Essential

Florida		*, which tourists enjoy visiting ,*		*has plenty of sunshine.*
SUBJ OF IND CLAUSE	+	**, DEP ADJ CLAUSE ,**	+	**PREDICATE OF IND CLAUSE**

Page 143

Dependent Adjective Clauses — Essential

The painting		*that Tom finished for his brother*		*looks professional.*
SUBJ OF IND CLAUSE	+	**DEP ADJ CLAUSE**	+	**PREDICATE OF IND CLAUSE**

Page 149

Recap